Game, Set, Laugh
Book of Tennis Cartoons

Featuring Cartoons From
Air Mail
The New Yorker
and more!

Front Cover illustration: Royston Robertson
Back Cover illustration: James Stevenson
Introduction: Bob Mankoff
Edited By: Darren Kornblut

Dedicated to Jennifer & Bea

Cartoon Collections, LLC
10 Grand Central, 29th Floor
New York, NY 10017

For cartoon licensing information visit www.cartoonstock.com
Create a personalized version of this book at www.cartoonstockgifts.com

First edition published 2024

Item # 49235
ISBN: 978-1-963079-19-7

Introduction

Welcome to a world where love means nothing, and yet, everything. This is the realm of tennis, a sport that serves up humor as often as it does aces. Within these pages you'll find a collection of cartoons that volley between the comically relatable and the hilariously absurd.

As the former cartoon editor for *The New Yorker*, I've seen my fair share of sketches that tickle the funny bone. But there's something uniquely whimsical about tennis—perhaps it's the grunts, the white attire, or the genteel clapping—that makes it a perfect backhand smash for humor.

Here, we've gathered the crème de la crème of tennis cartoons. Whether you're a fan of the sport or someone who thinks 'break point' is a term for when your patience snaps, there's something in here for you. From the baseline banter to the net worth of chuckles, each cartoon is a match point in mirth.

Prepare to embark on a delightful journey through the world of tennis, where the serve is only as good as the punchline and the lob can be just as unexpected as a well-timed gag.

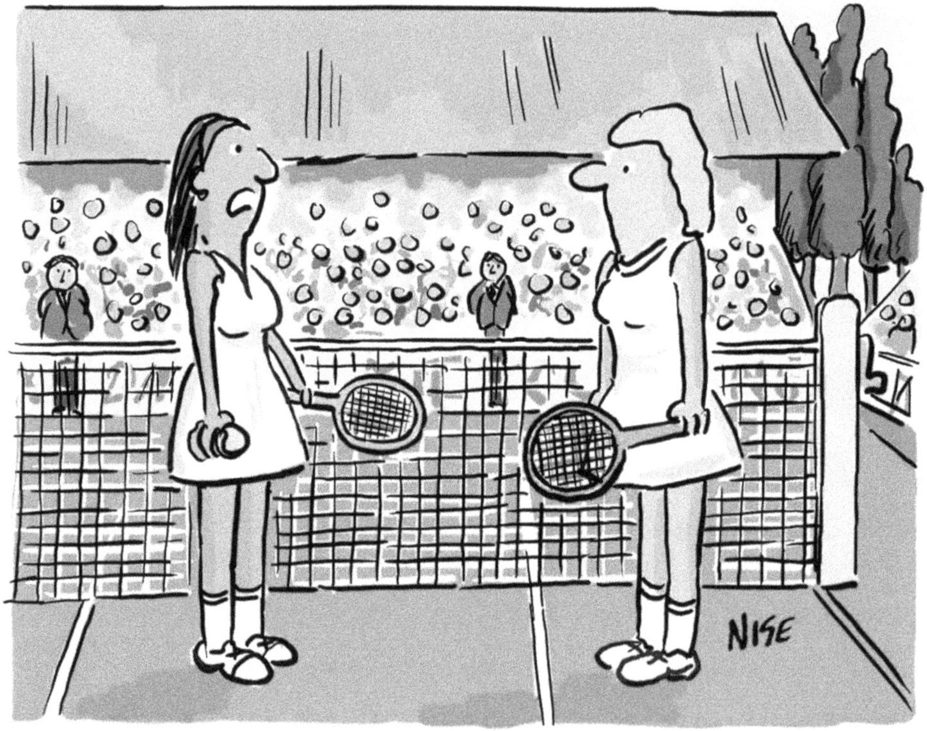
NISE

"It's not a doubles match – you're my opponent!"

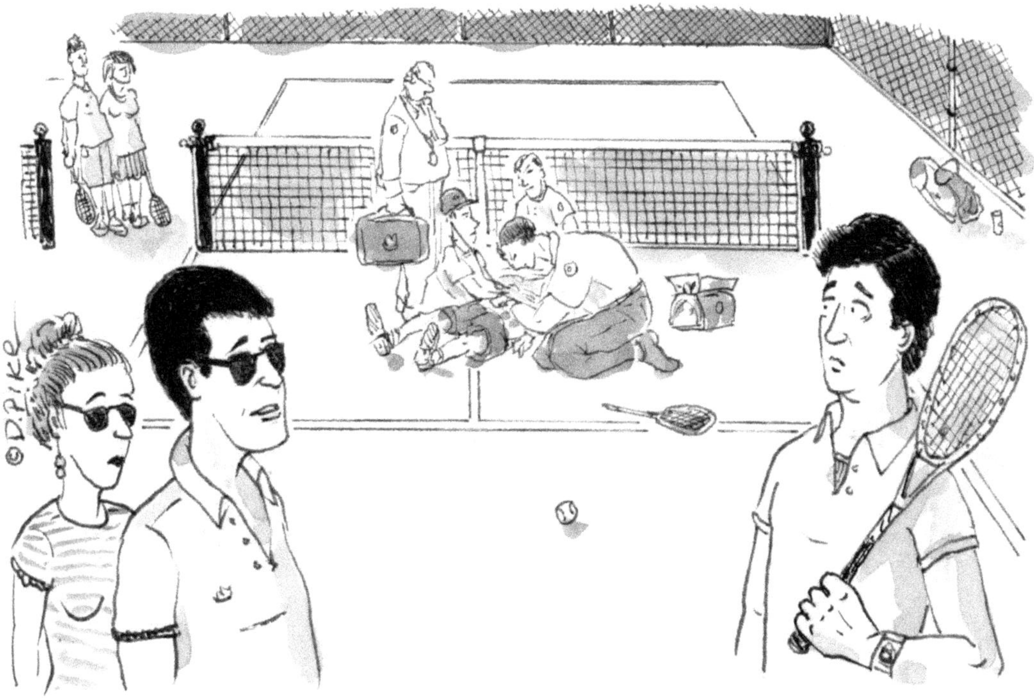
©D.PIKE

"Any idea how much longer you'll be?"

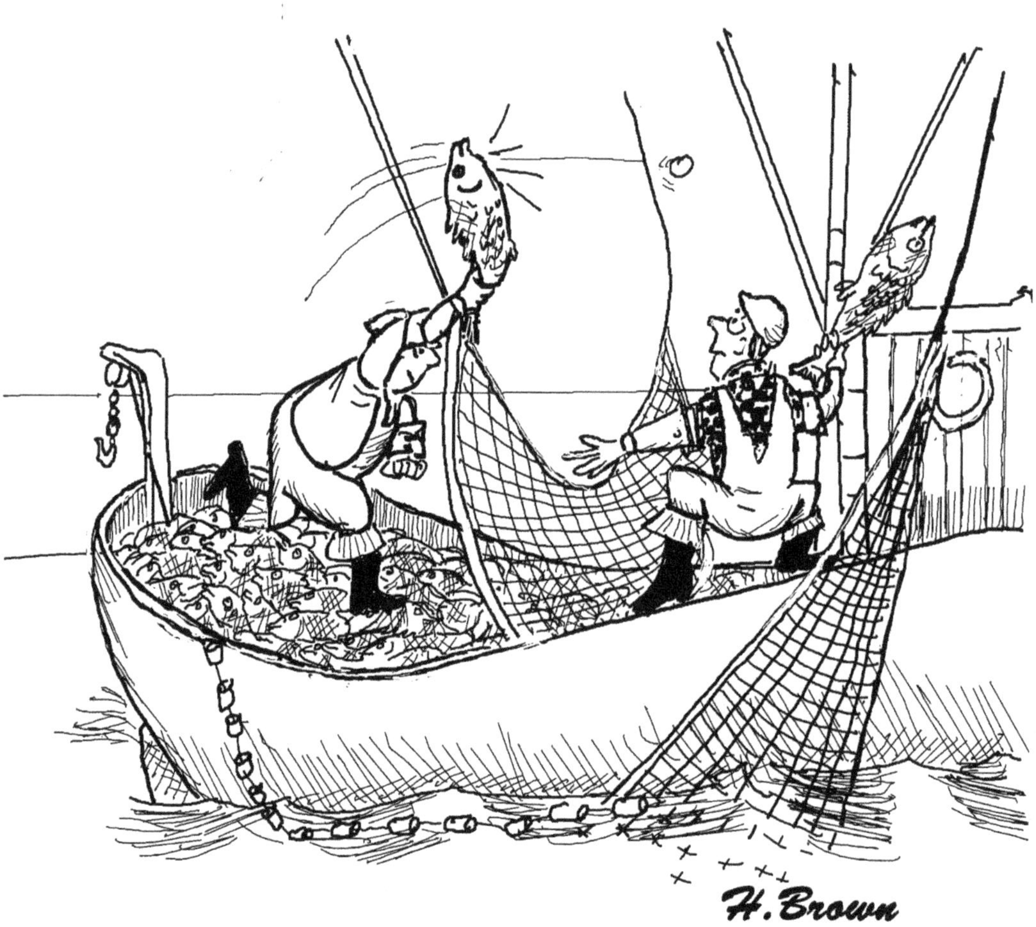
H. Brown

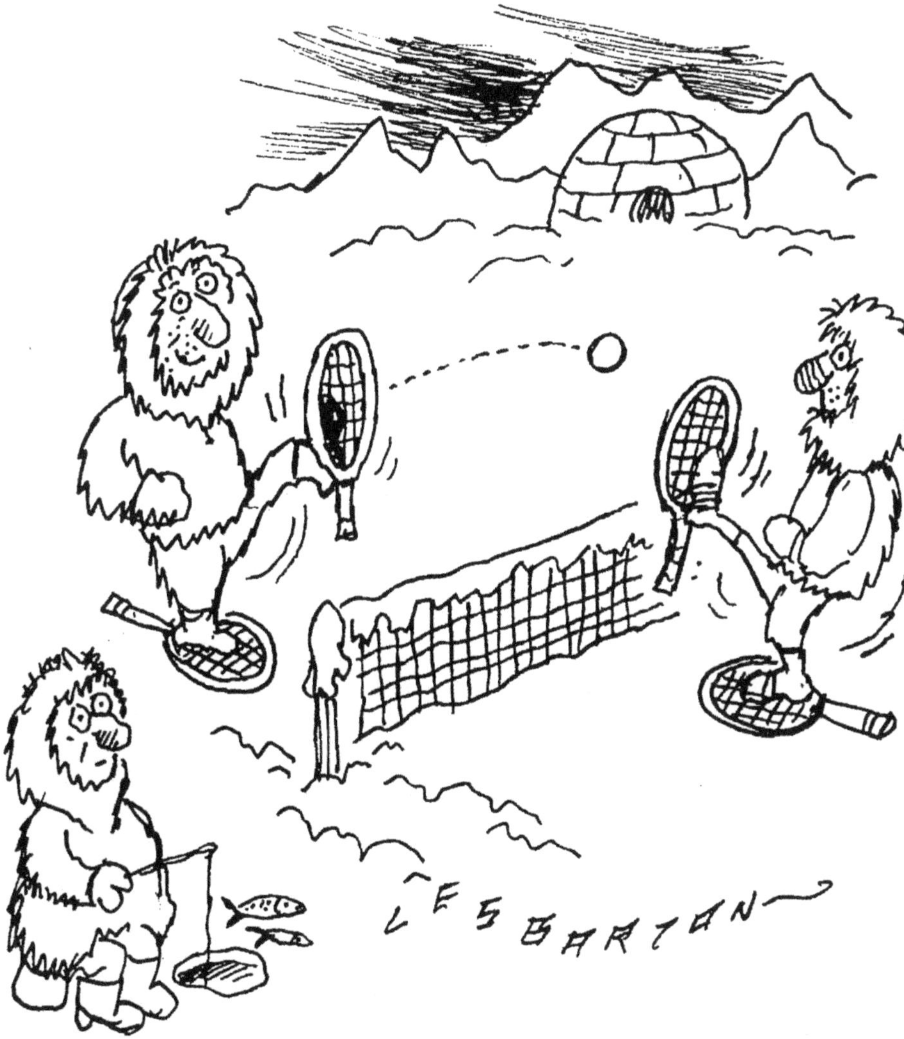
LES BARTON

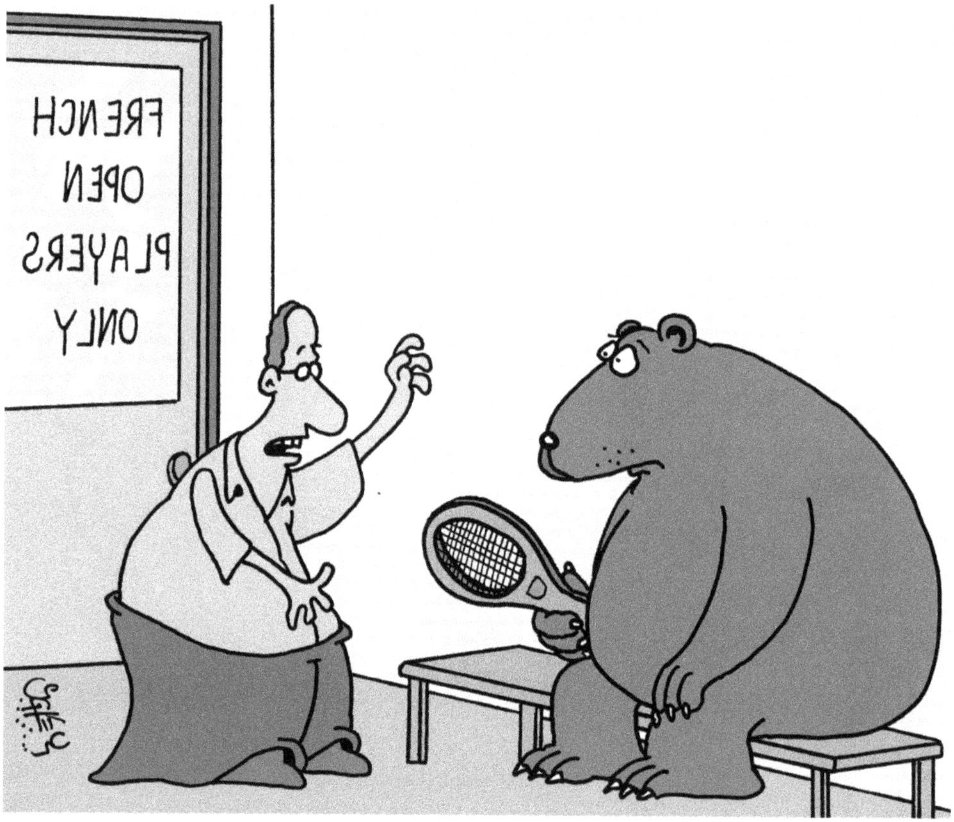
FRENCH
OPEN
PLAYERS
ONLY

"You can still win this! Try using your forehand like you would if you were catching salmon from the river!"

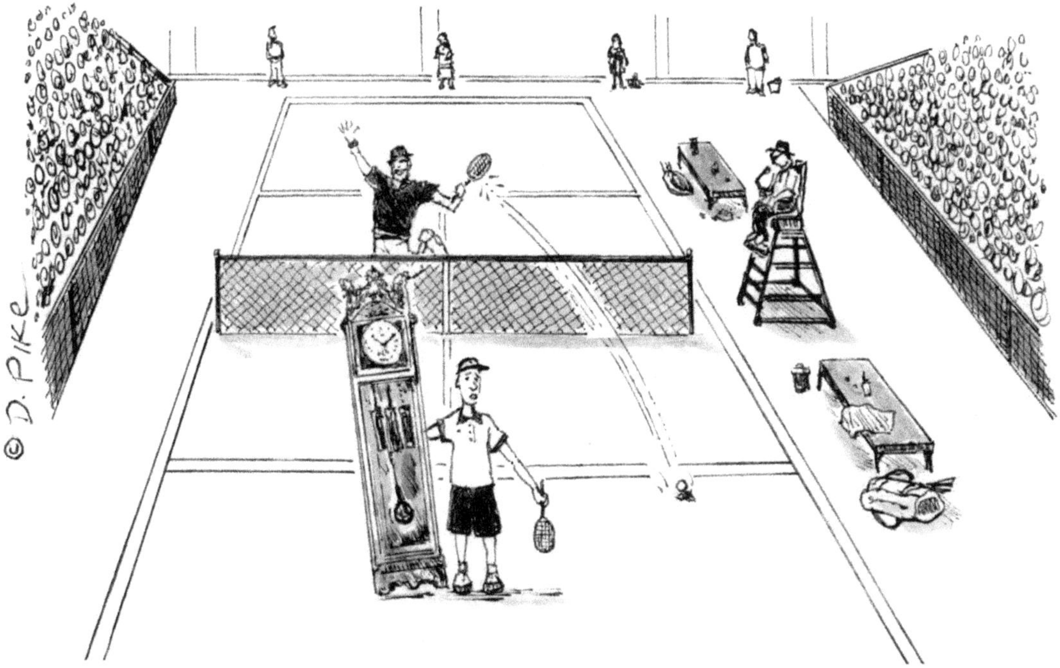
© D. PIKE

"Why couldn't my agent get me an endorsement deal with a wrist watch maker, like every other tennis player?"

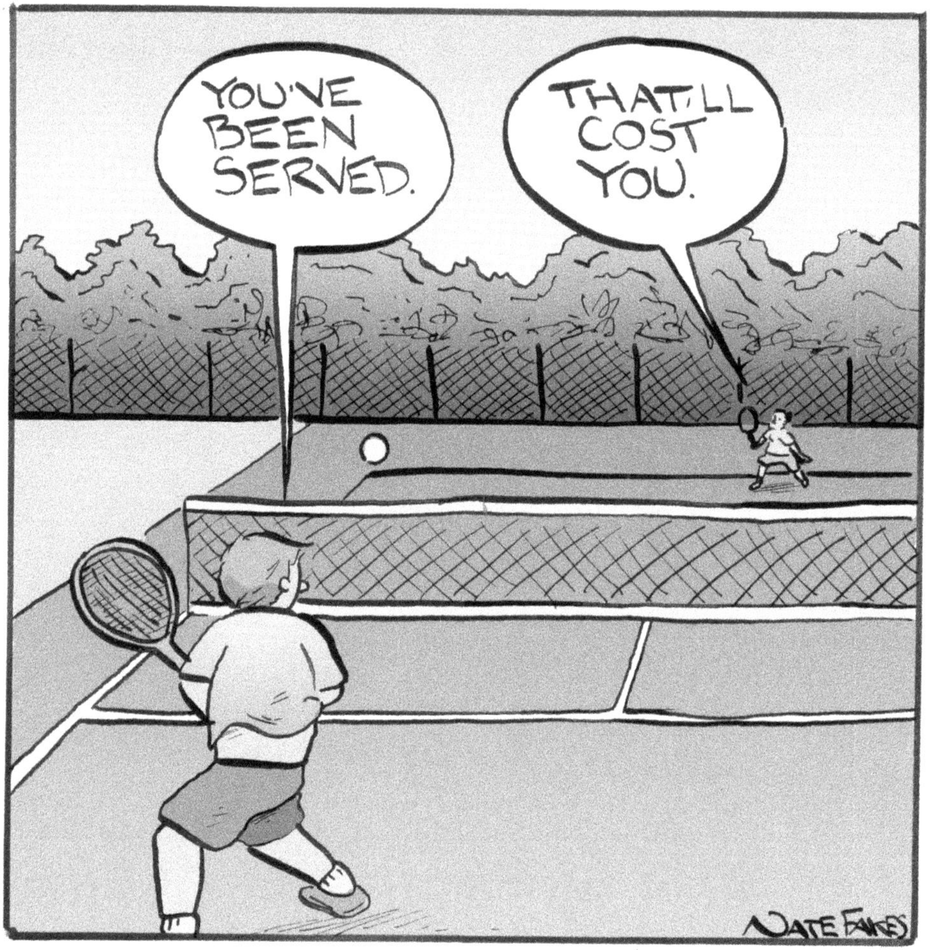
YOU'VE BEEN SERVED.
THAT'LL COST YOU.
NATE FAKES

"Lawyers Playing Tennis"

"That should keep him off our backs for a while."

"His serve is excellent, his forehand is strong, his backhand and net game are coming along well, but he needs a louder grunt."

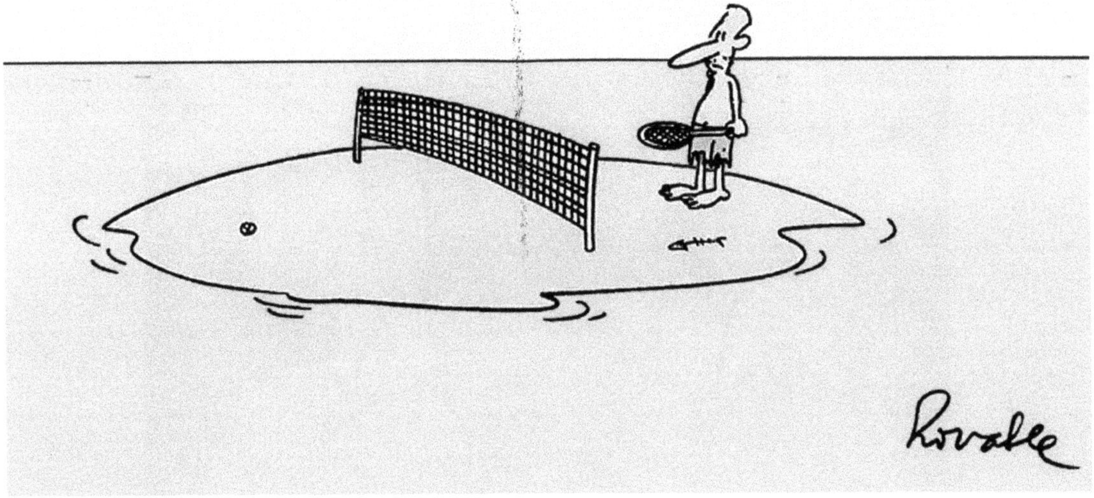
Kovalle

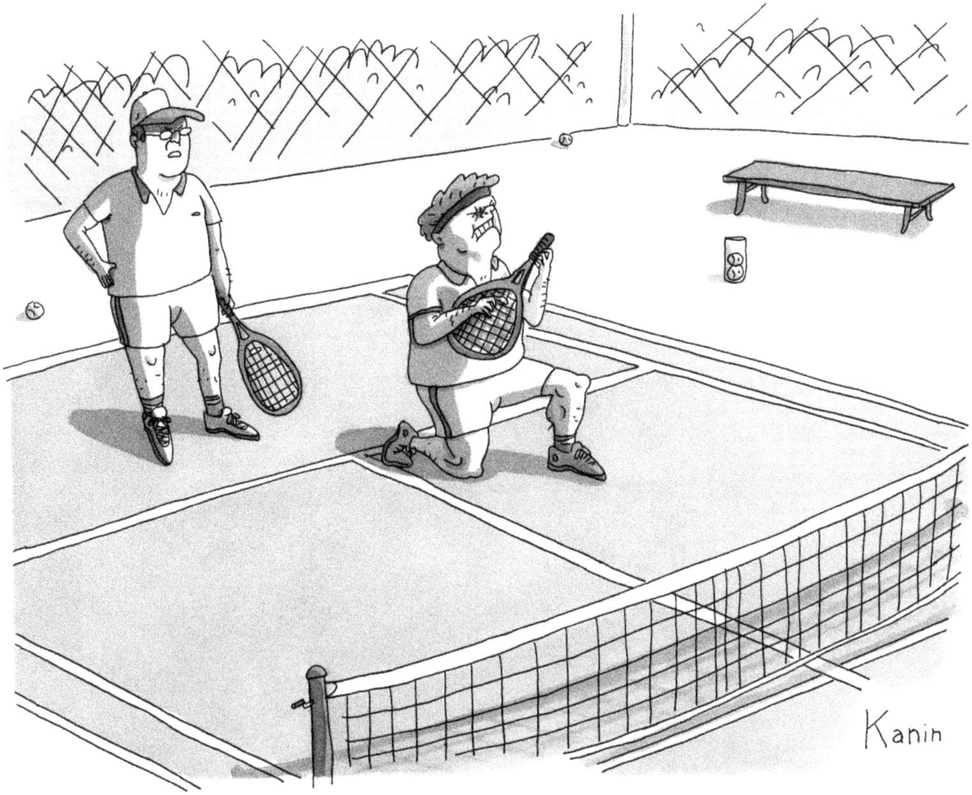
Kanin

"You can't take a solo after every serve."

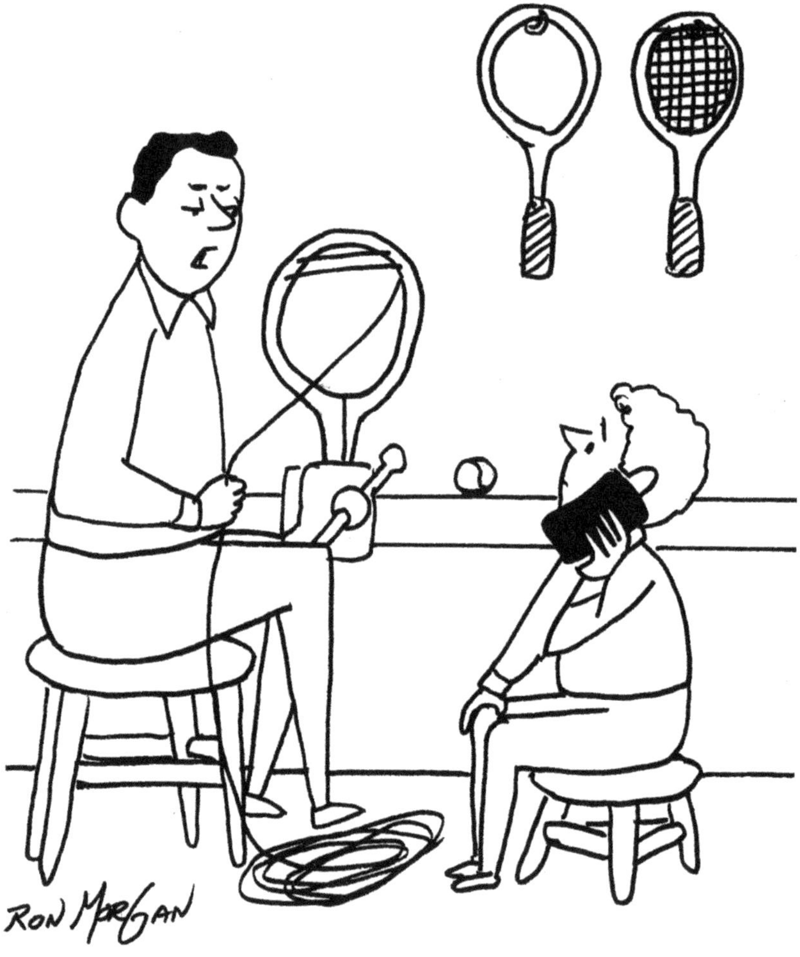
RON MORGAN

"I'm restringing a racquet, not 'racketeering'!"

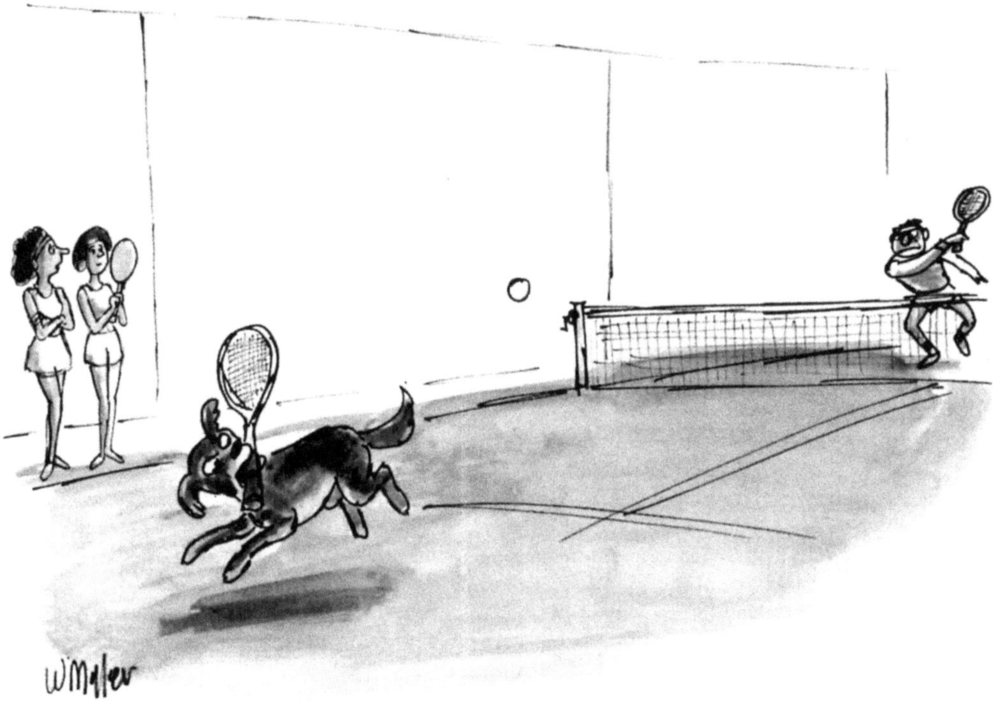
W.Miller

"It's kind of a shame, really. Before tennis they used to be the best of friends."

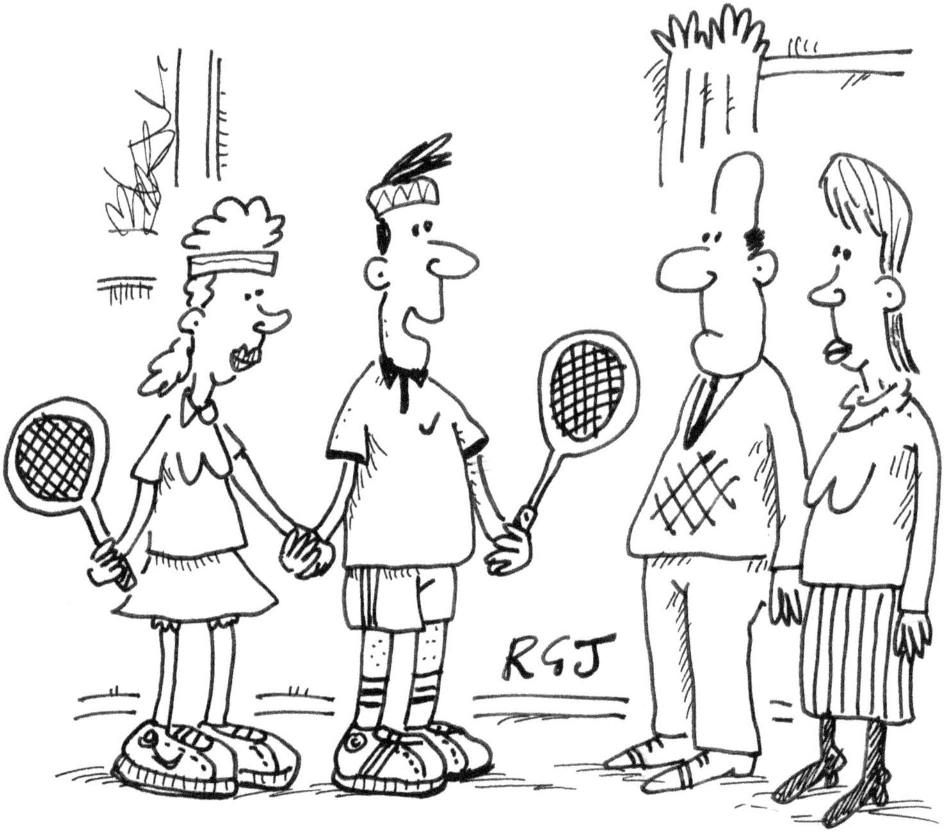
RGJ

"We met over the net."

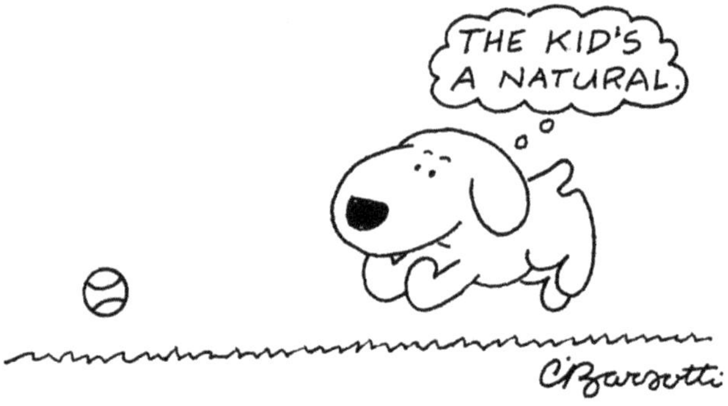
THE KID'S
A NATURAL.
CBarsotti

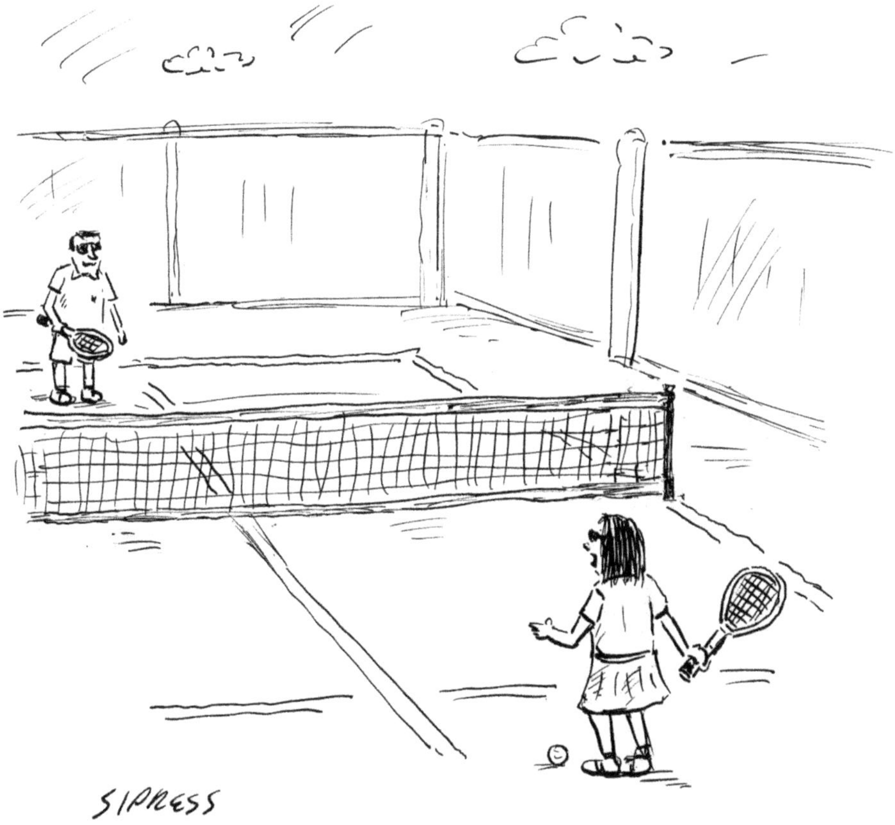
SIPRESS

"Can you please just say 'Fault', and quit adding 'is not in our stars but in ourselves'."

"Let this be a lesson...never laugh at someone
who double-faults match point."

"Just to set the record straight, I'm leaving you because you never turn your body
to the net, you don't have a smooth swing, and because your forehand,
backhand, and volley are inadequate!"

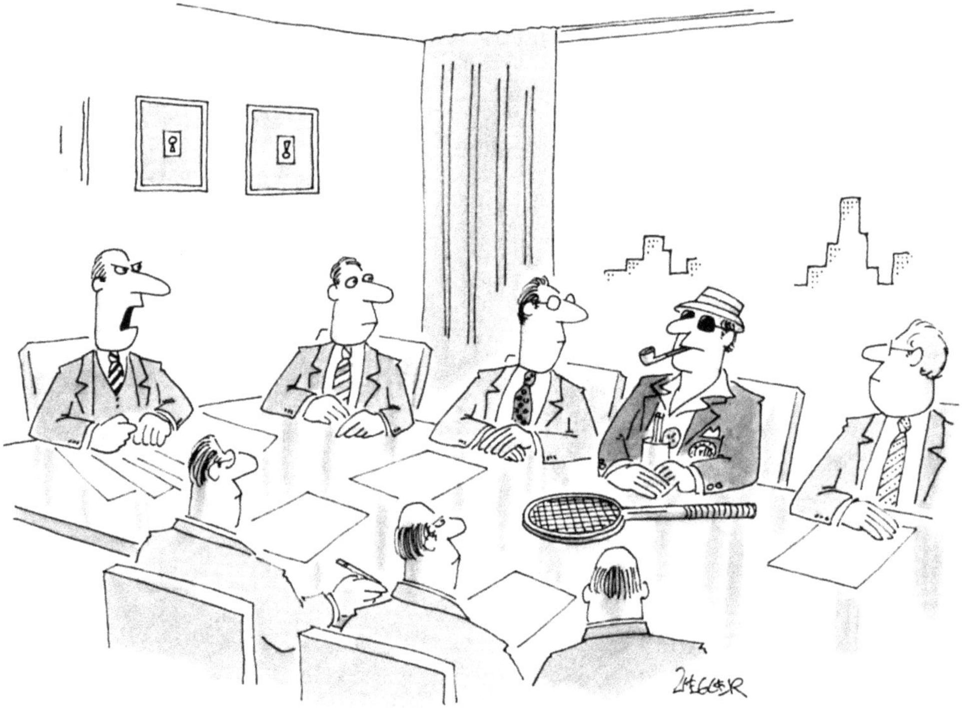
ZIEGLER

"You're on the forty-ninth floor now, Mr. Dowd. Up here, the world no longer revolves around you."

"You need to take a break from
watching too many tennis matches."

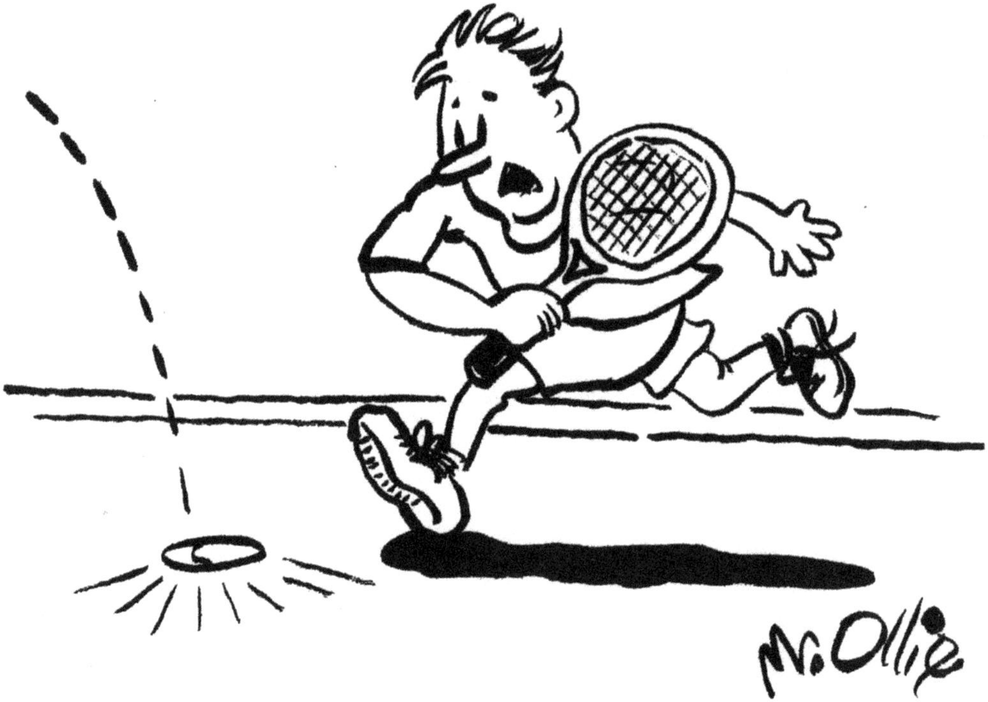
Mr.Ollie

"These balls are a little flat."

"The other way. Face
the other way, Charlie."

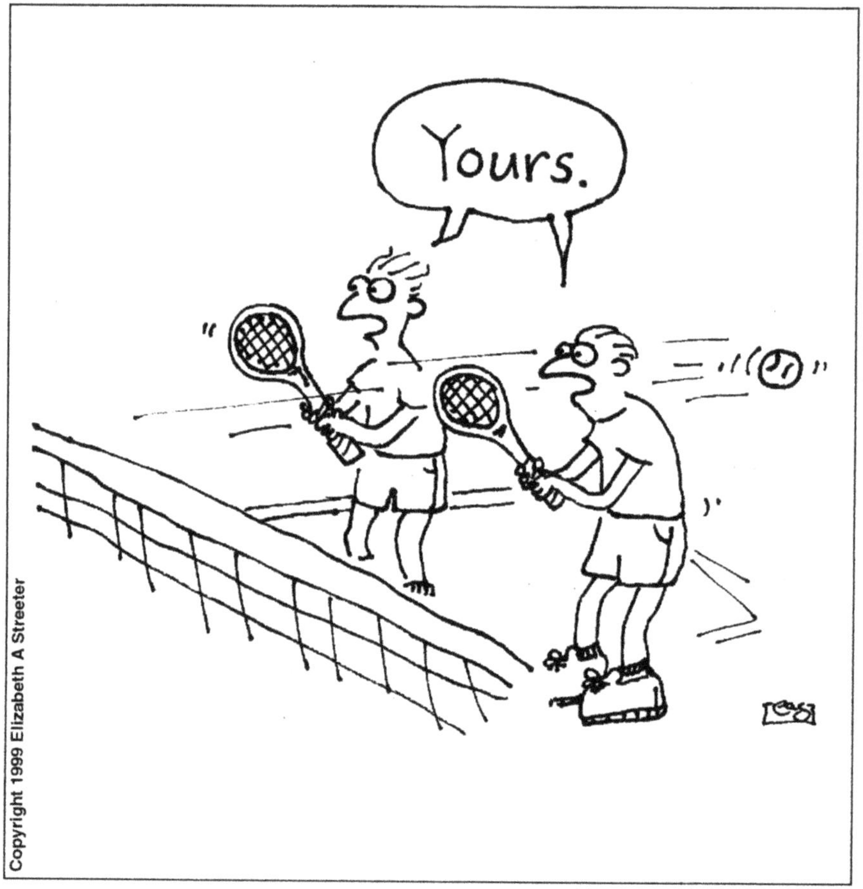
Yours.
Copyright 1999 Elizabeth A Streeter

"Middle managers play tennis."

"Hey, Mister, can my dog play with one
of your tennis balls?"

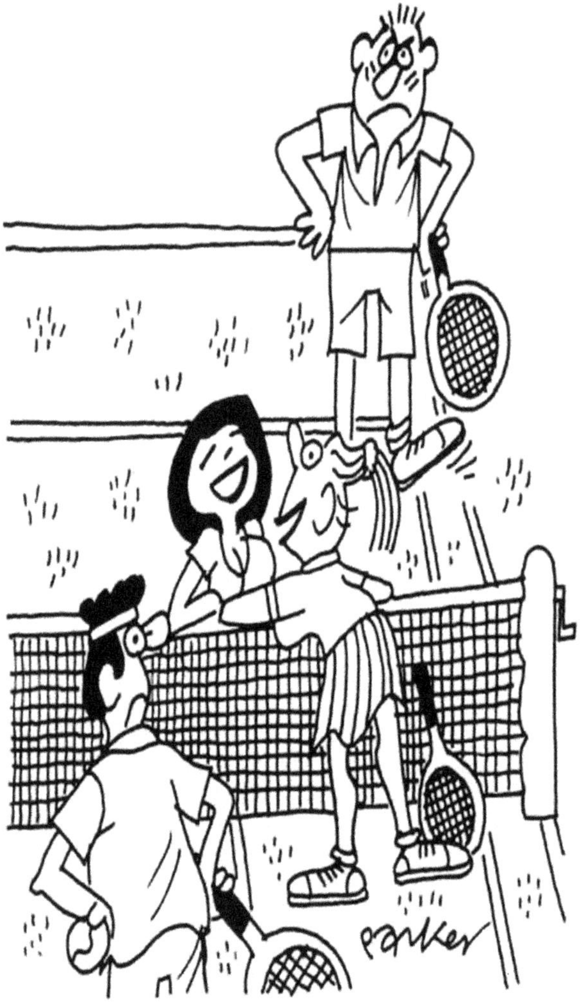
Parker

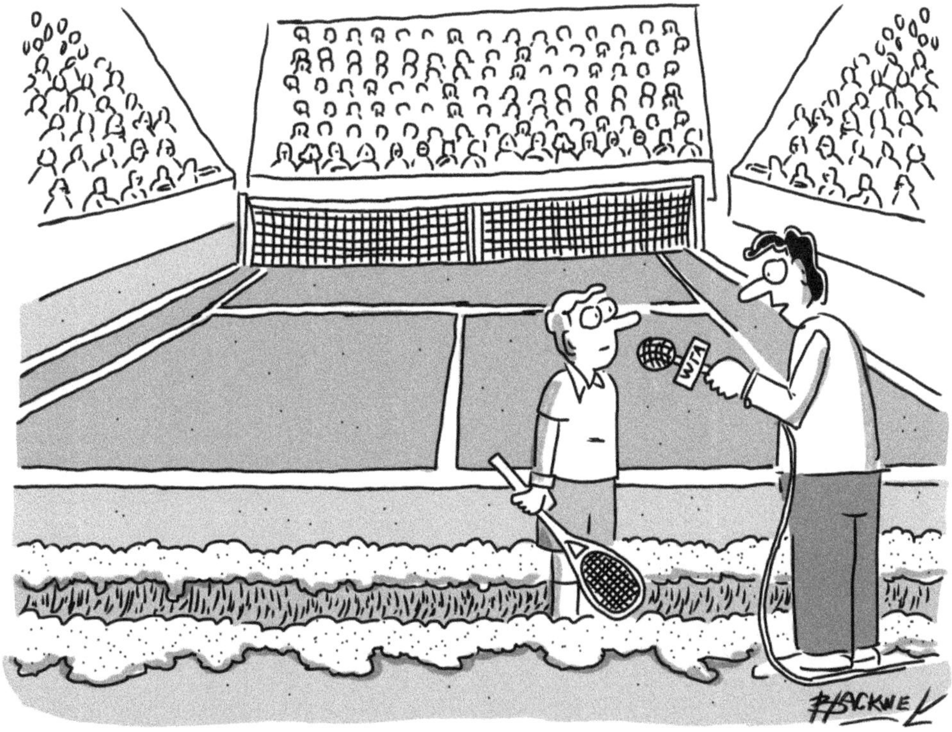
WTA

"How do you respond to critics who say you only play the backcourt?"

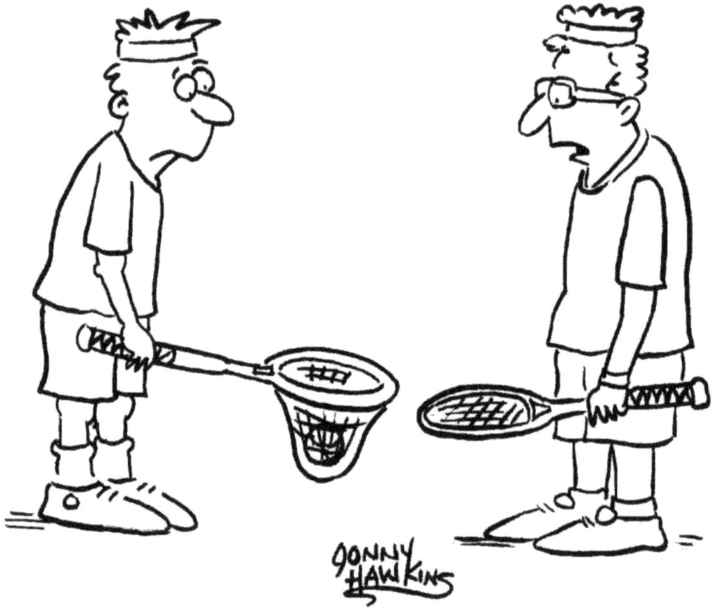
JONNY HAWKINS

"I'd get the strings tightened."

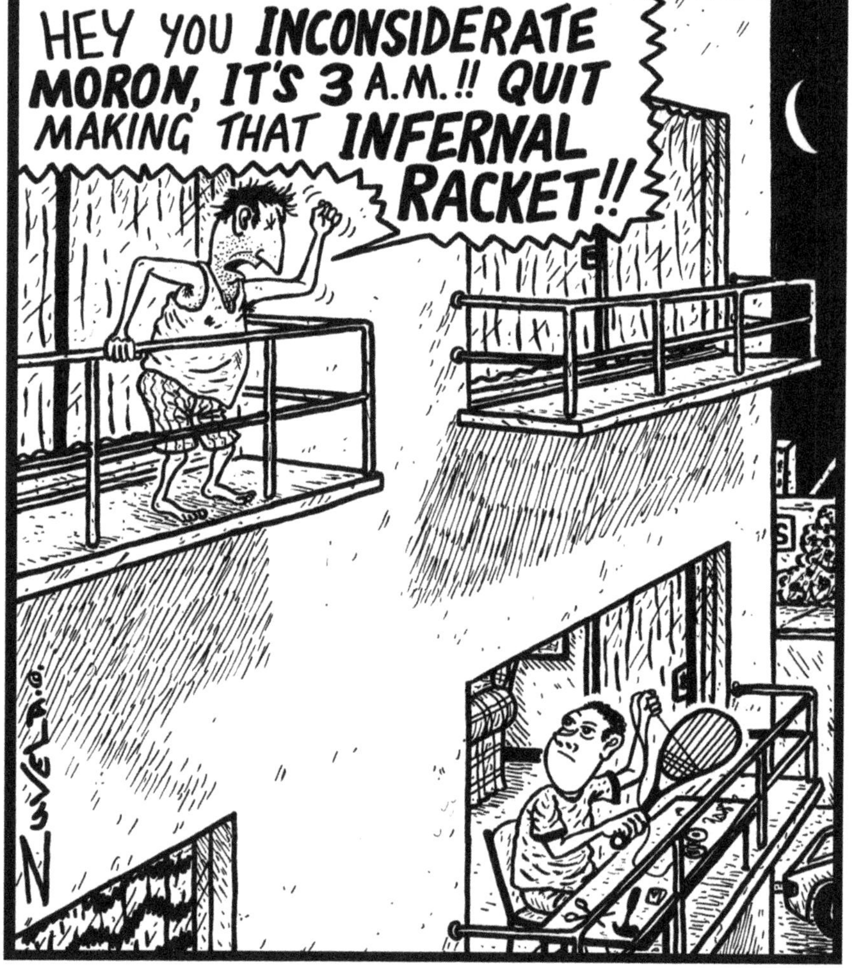
HEY YOU INCONSIDERATE MORON, IT'S 3 A.M.!! QUIT MAKING THAT INFERNAL RACKET!!

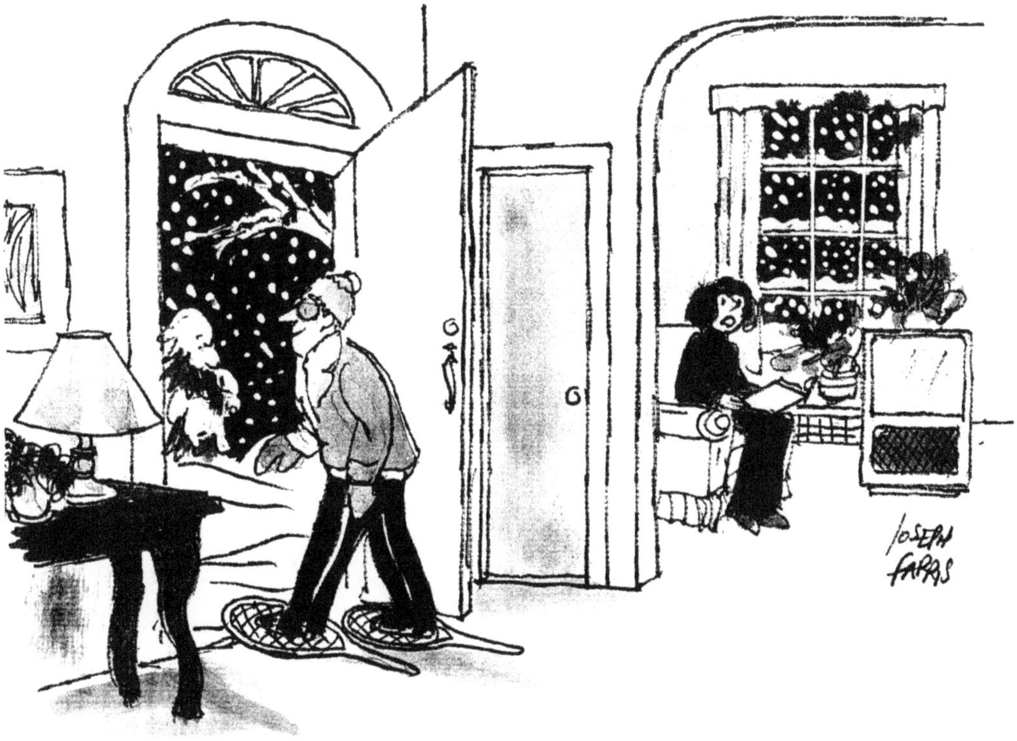
JOSEPH FARRIS

"Are you crazy? How are you going to run in the snow?"

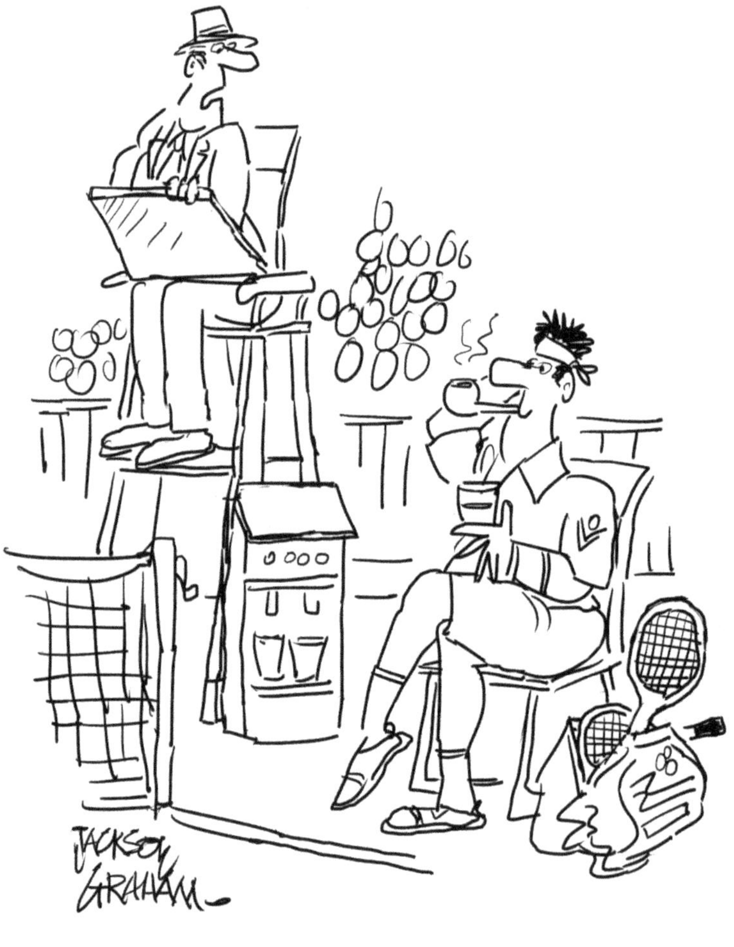
JACKSON GRAHAM

"Time!!"

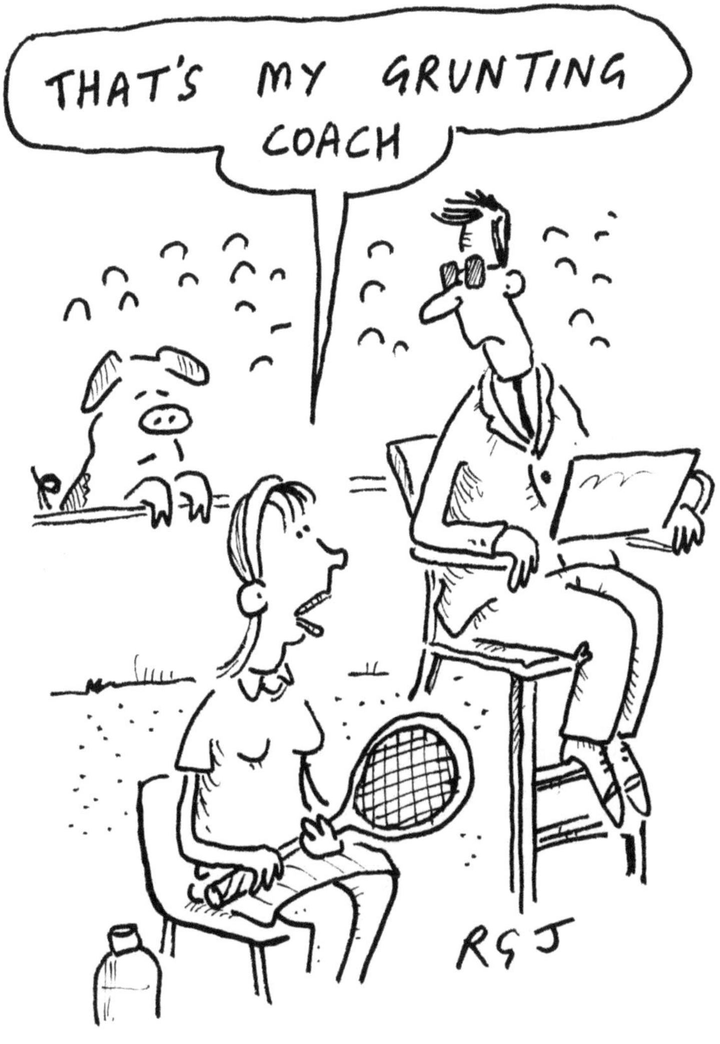
THAT'S MY GRUNTING COACH
RGJ

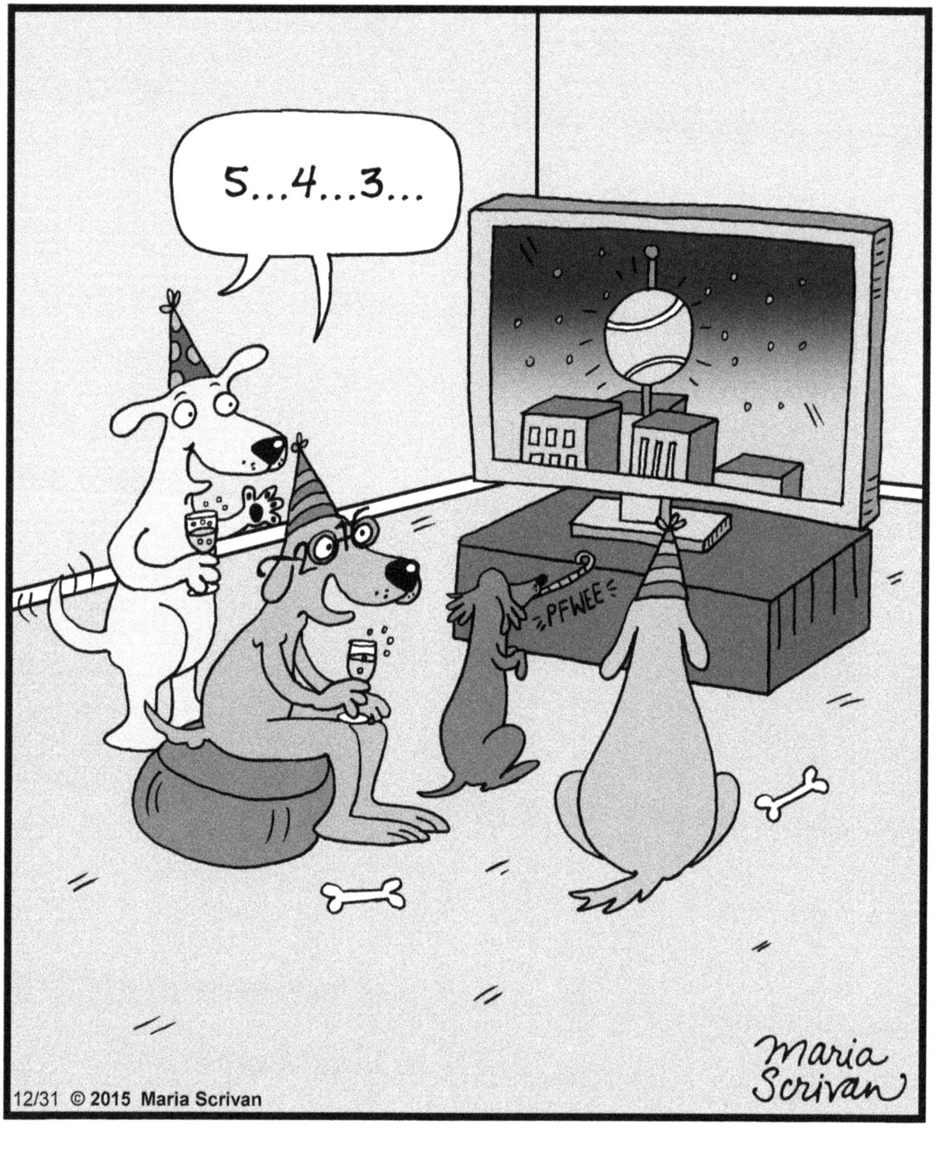
5...4...3...
PFWEE
Maria Scrivan
12/31 © 2015 Maria Scrivan

*"Wow, that's the worst case of tennis elbow
I've seen this year!"*

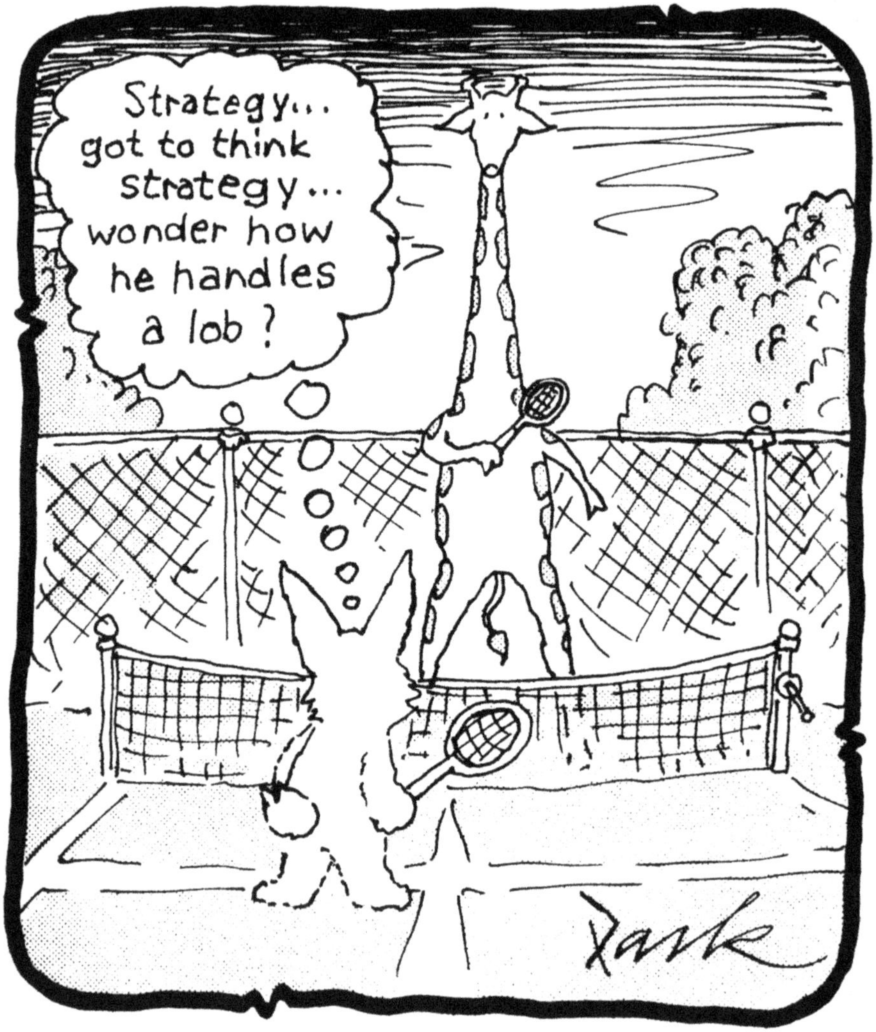
Strategy... got to think strategy... wonder how he handles a lob?
Park

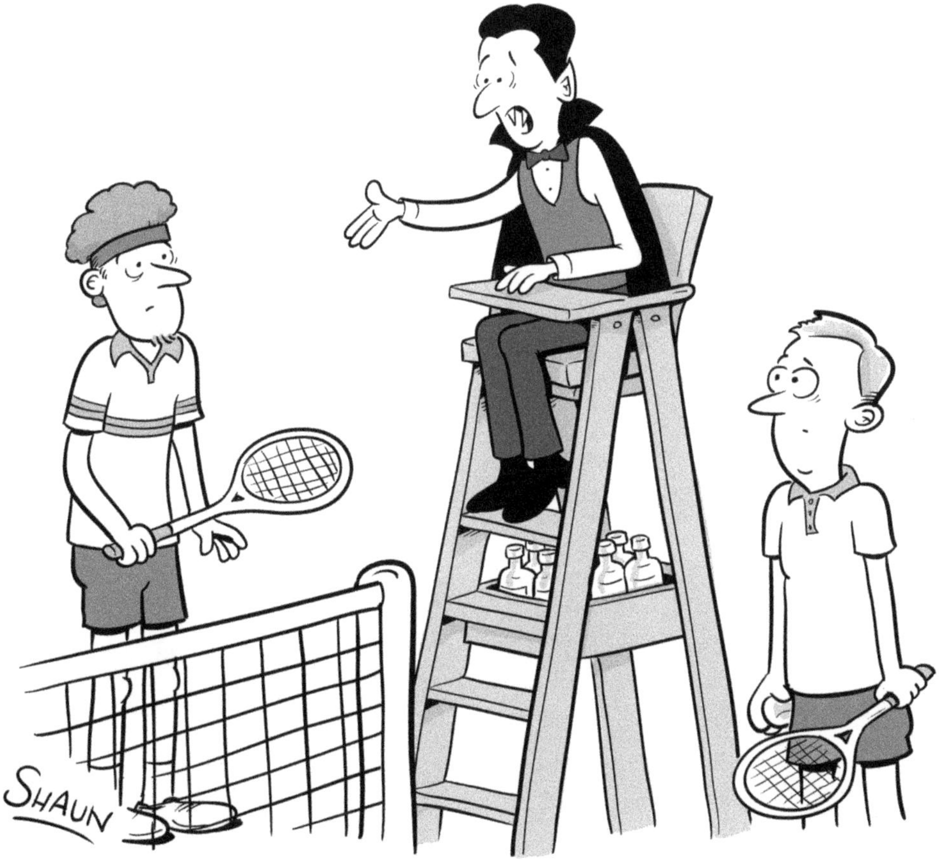
SHAUN

"Yeah, there was a mix up at the job center."

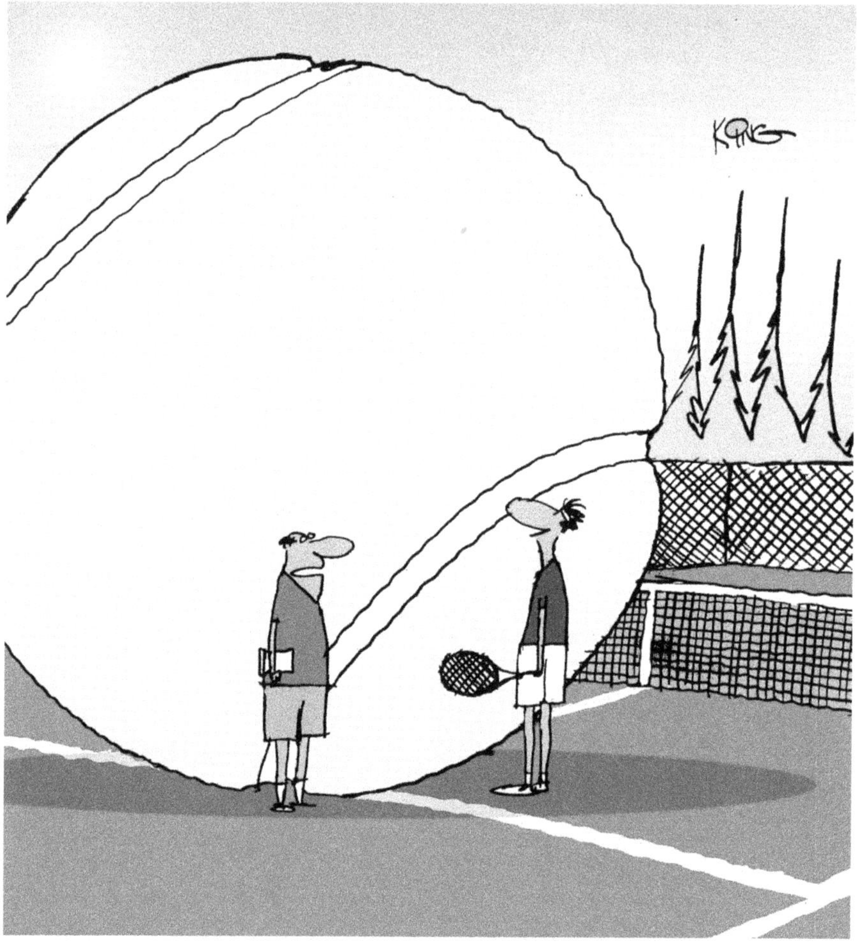
KING

"Your serves are a little weak. Practicing with this ball should solve that problem."

"Ballboy! Please wait until
the rally ends!"

"That's 12 games in a row. As my best friend, it wouldn't kill you to let me win one every once in awhile."

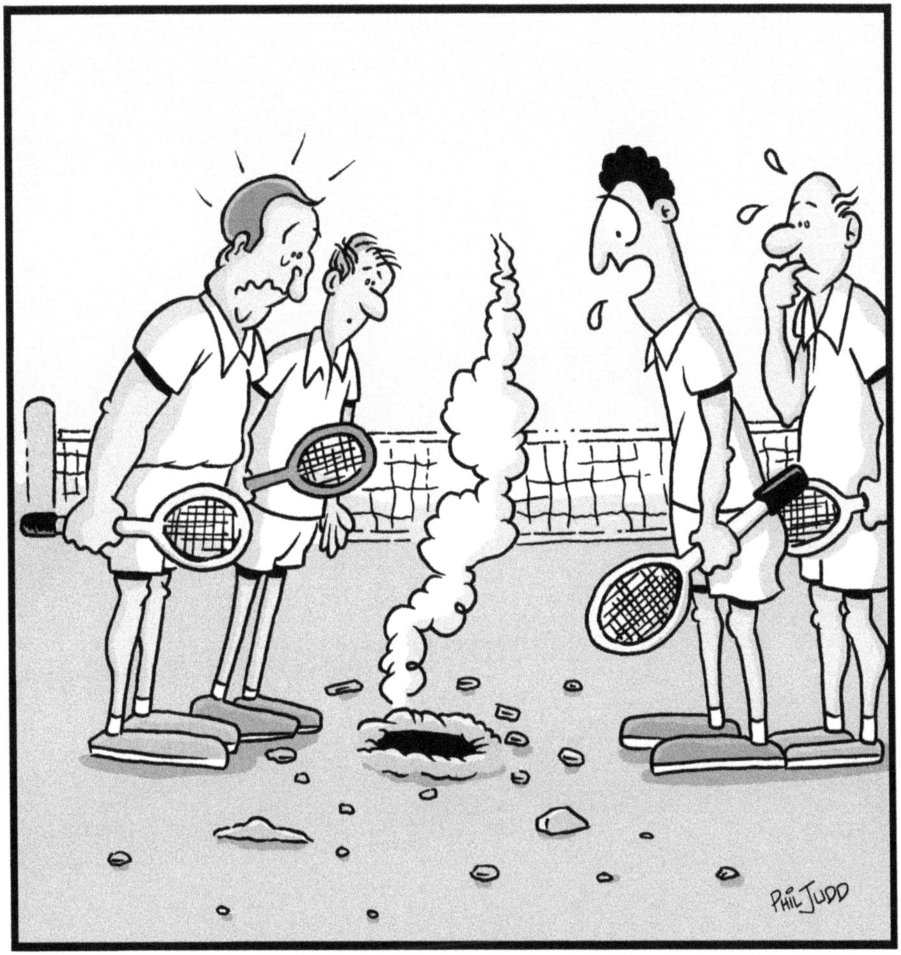
PHIL JUDD

"Now, that's what I call a smash!"

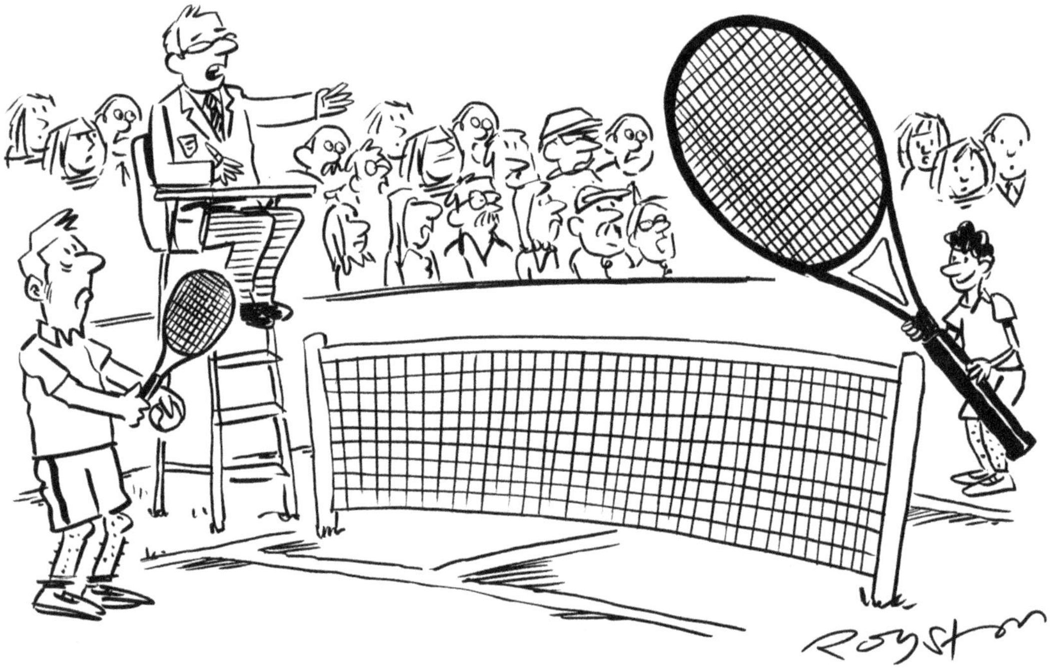
ROYSTON

"Advantage."

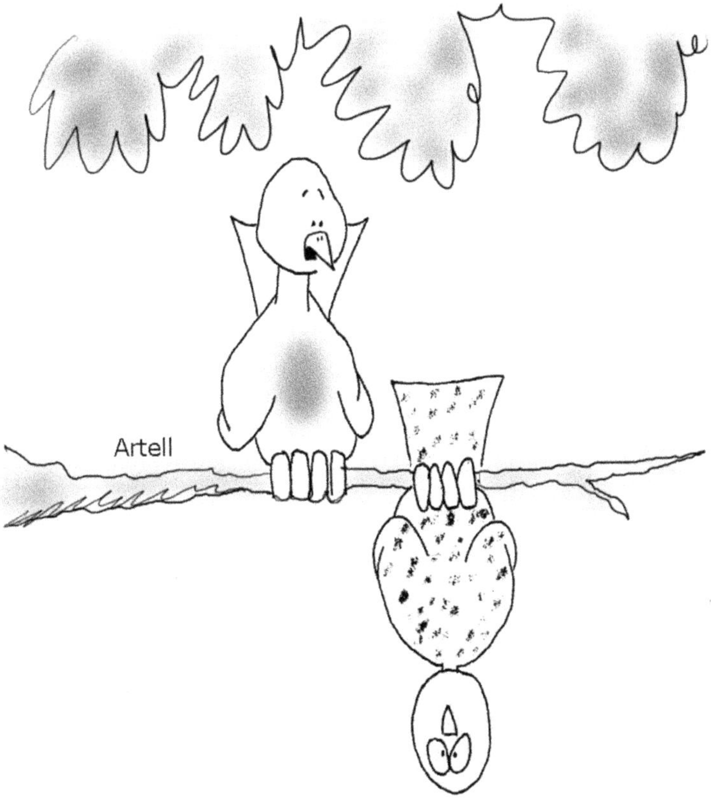
Artell

"You need to work on your grip."

"Genuine enthusiasm."

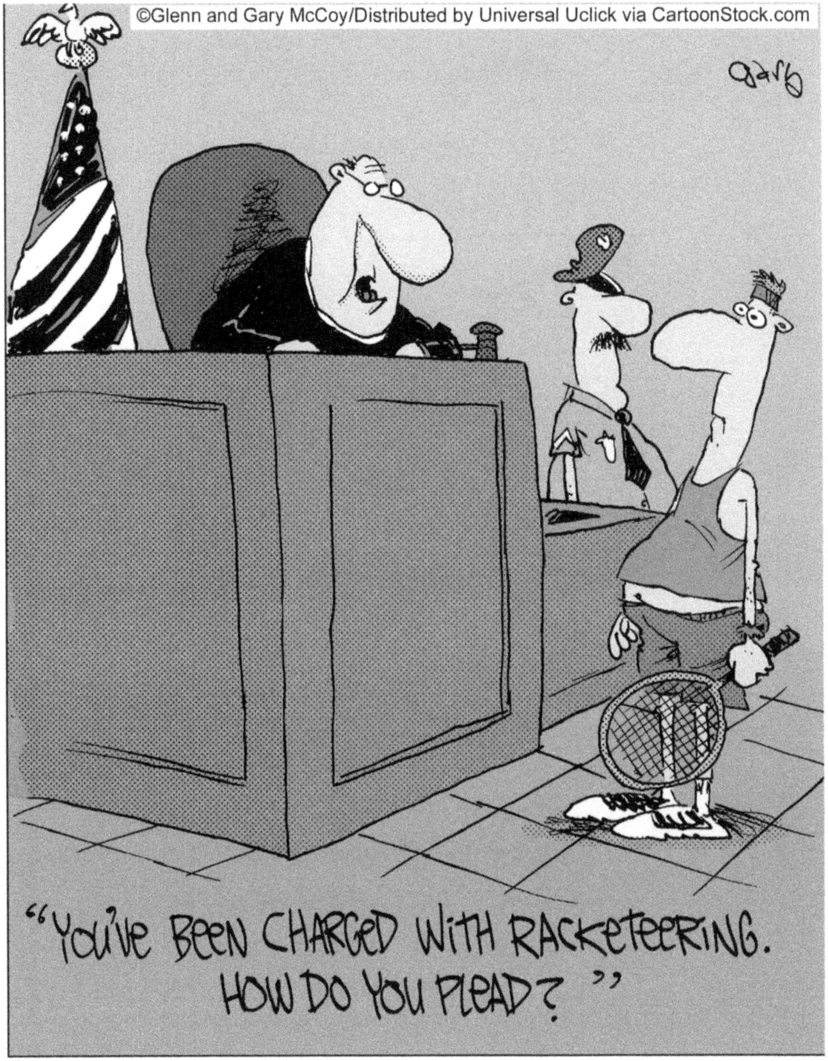
©Glenn and Gary McCoy/Distributed by Universal Uclick via CartoonStock.com
Gary
"YOU'VE BEEN CHARGED WITH RACKETEERING.
HOW DO YOU PLEAD?"

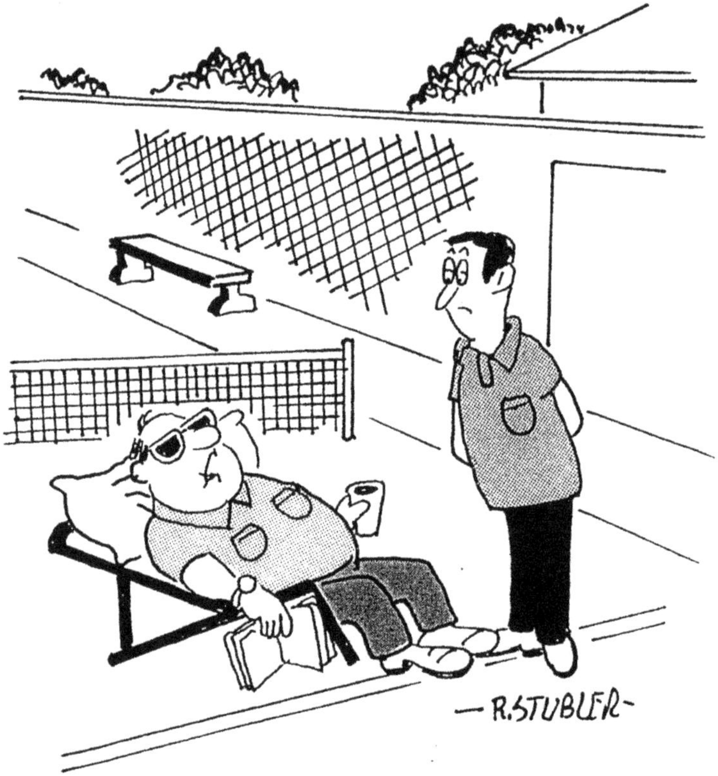
R.STUBLER

"I follow my doctor's orders religiously. He said for me to spend two hours a day on the tennis court."

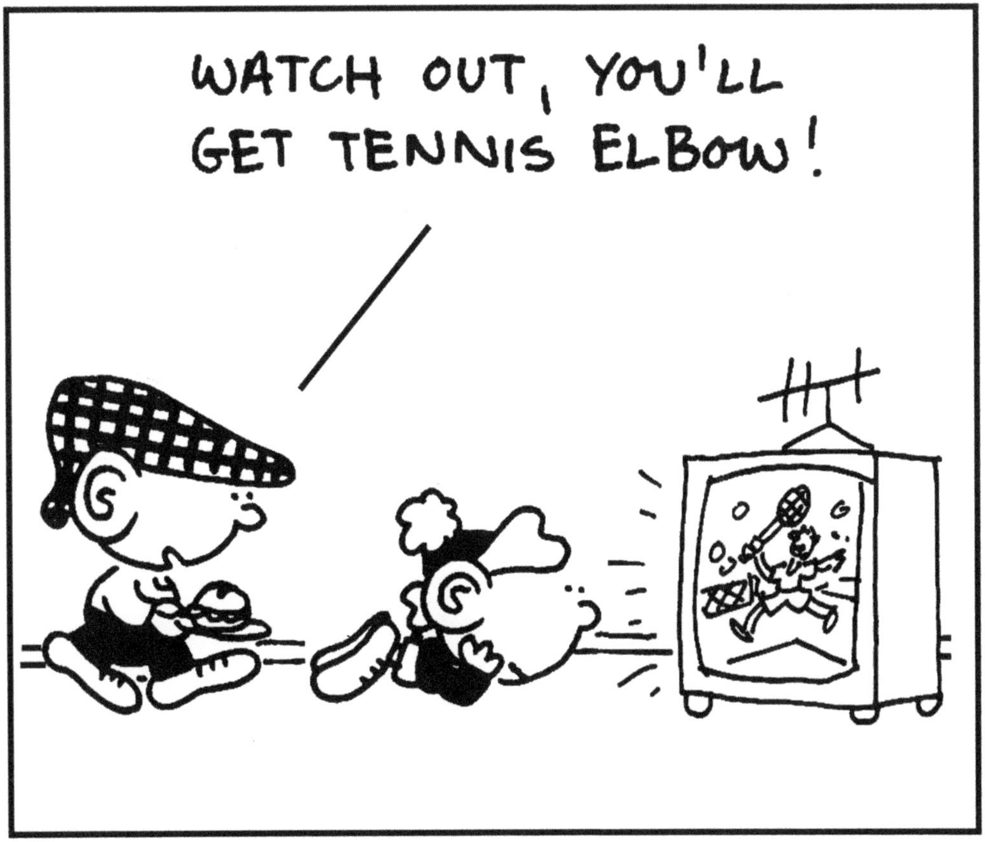
WATCH OUT, YOU'LL GET TENNIS ELBOW!

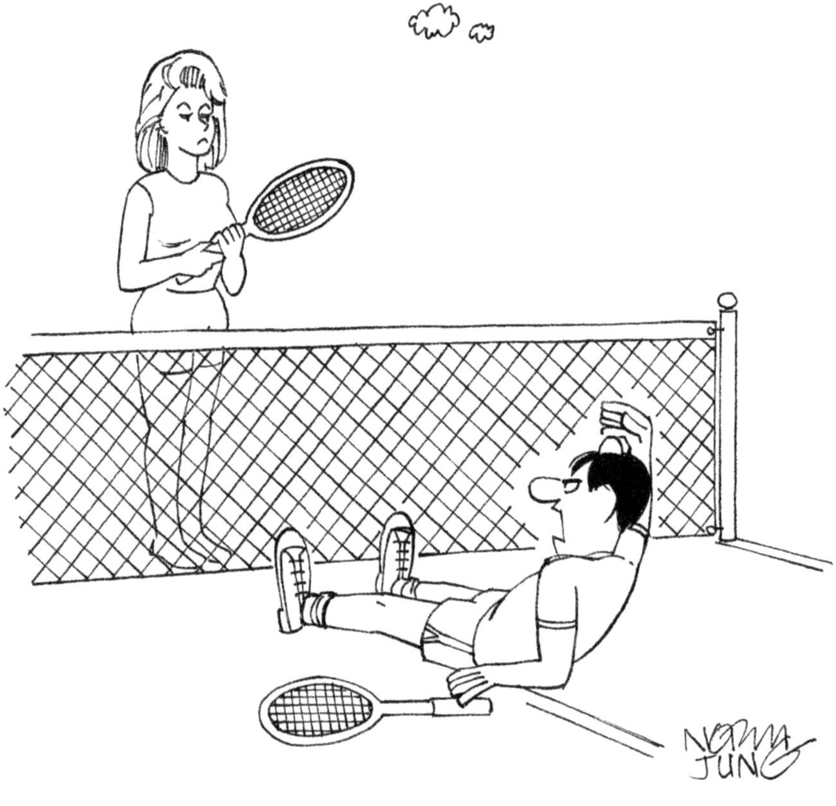
NORMA
JUNG

"Look dear, why don't you just lob the ball over until you get the hang of the game?"

"It's not doubles. That's his agent back there."

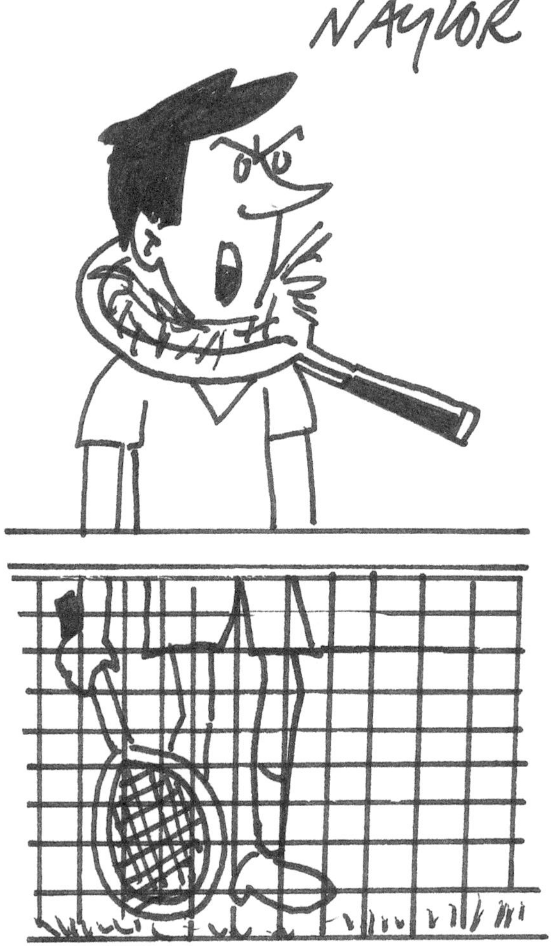
NAYLOR

"A handshake is customary!"

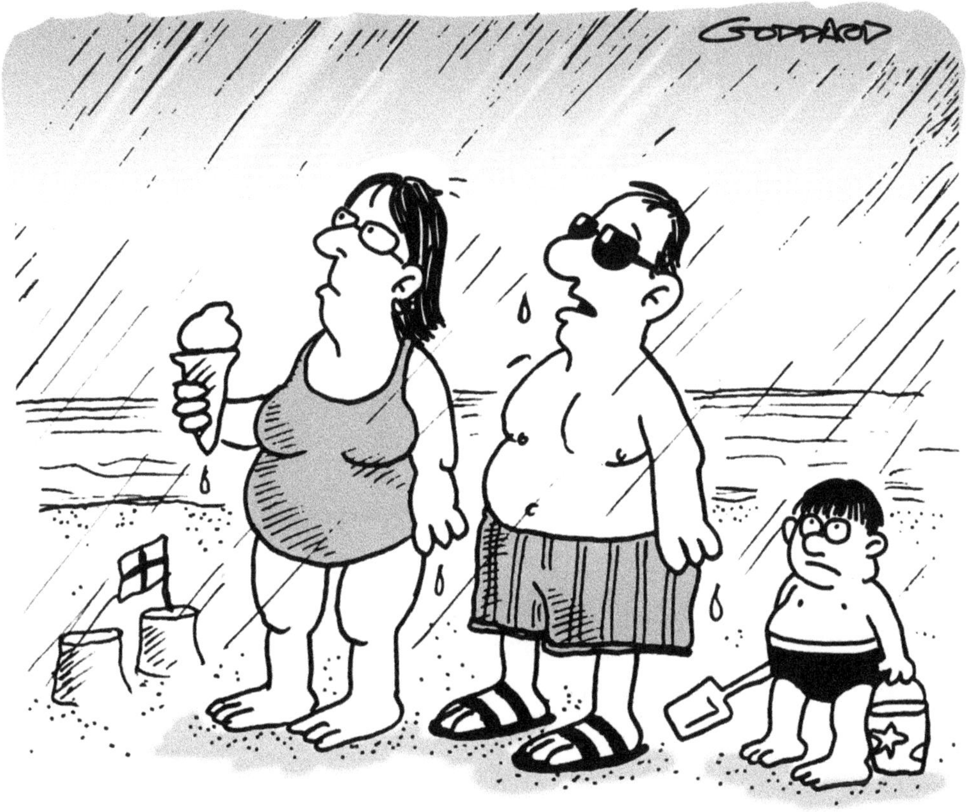
GODDARD

"Is it Wimbledon fortnight already?"

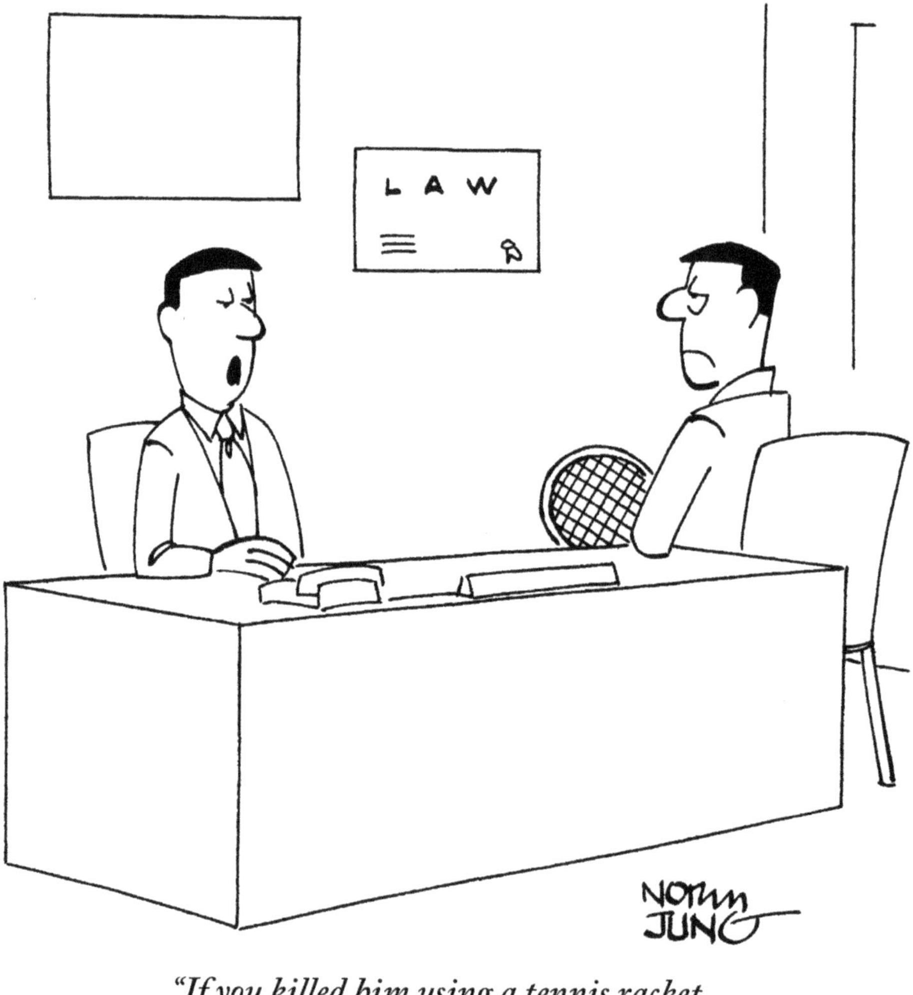
LAW
NORM
JUNG

"If you killed him using a tennis racket, you need a sports lawyer."

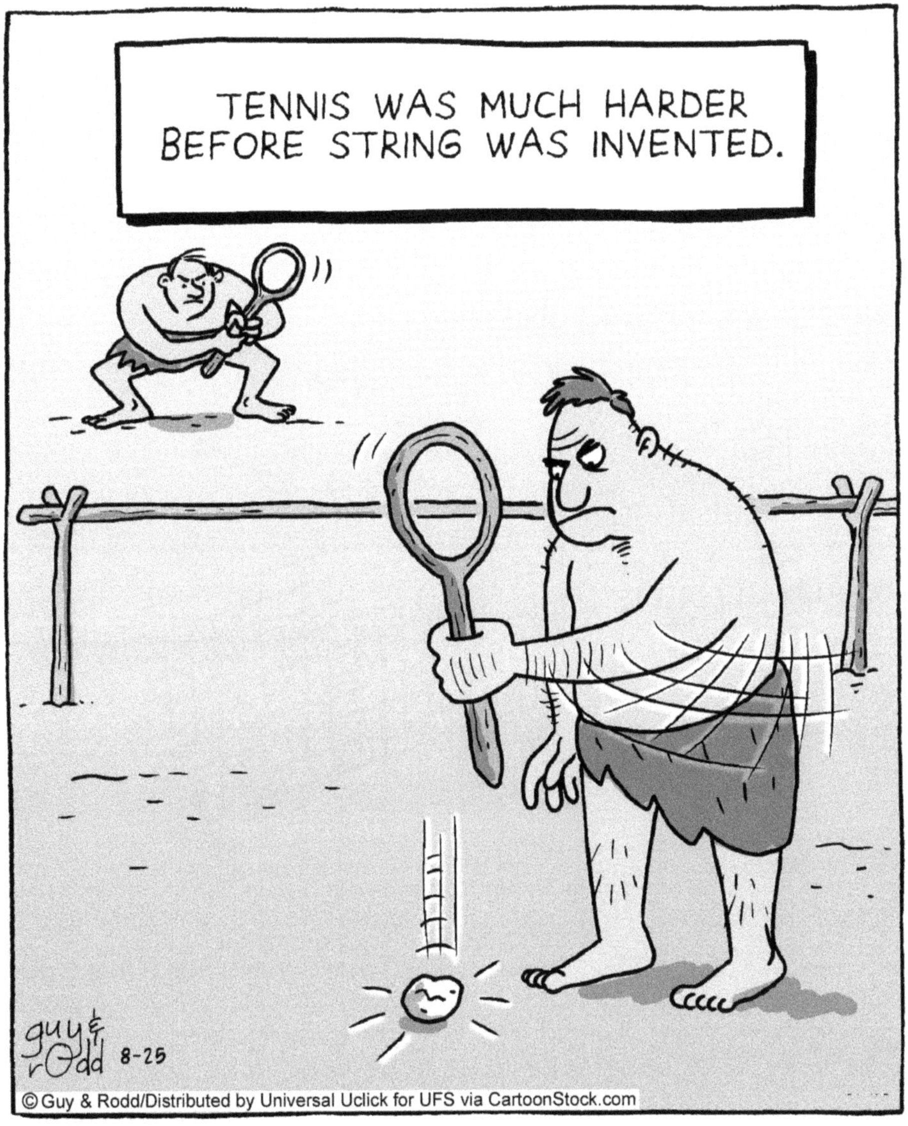
TENNIS WAS MUCH HARDER BEFORE STRING WAS INVENTED.
guy & rOdd 8-25

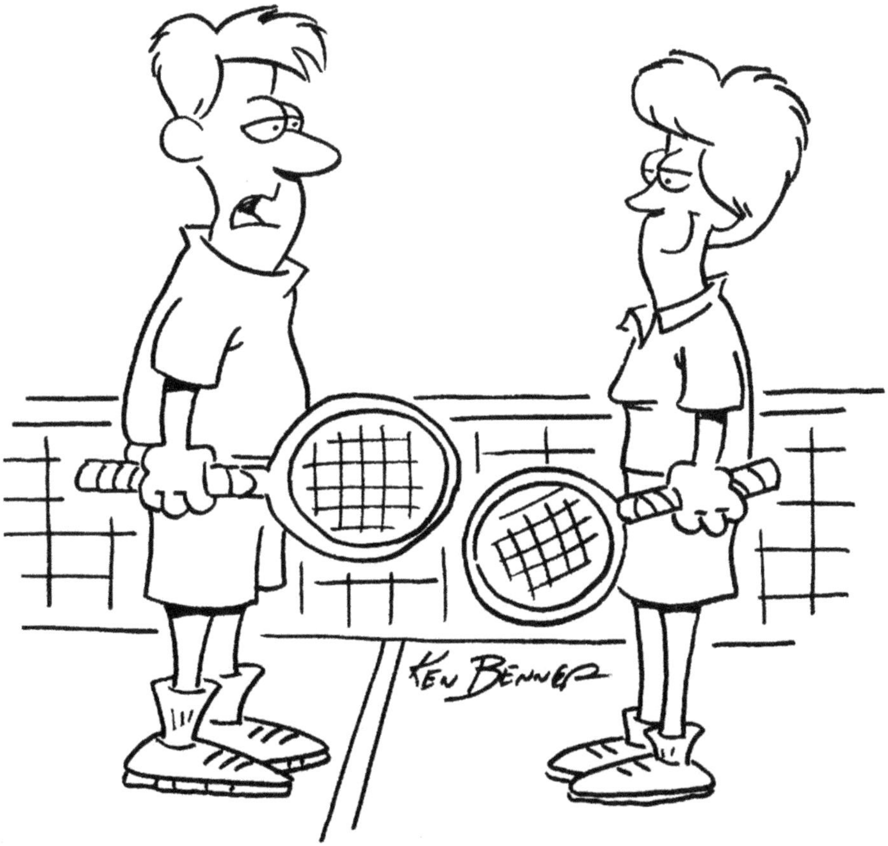
KEN BENNER

"I'm not playing games anymore..
especially if you keep beating me."

"I'm really sorry, Mr. Thompson... it seems I got
the chalk mixed up with the birdseed!"

THE OFF-SEASON

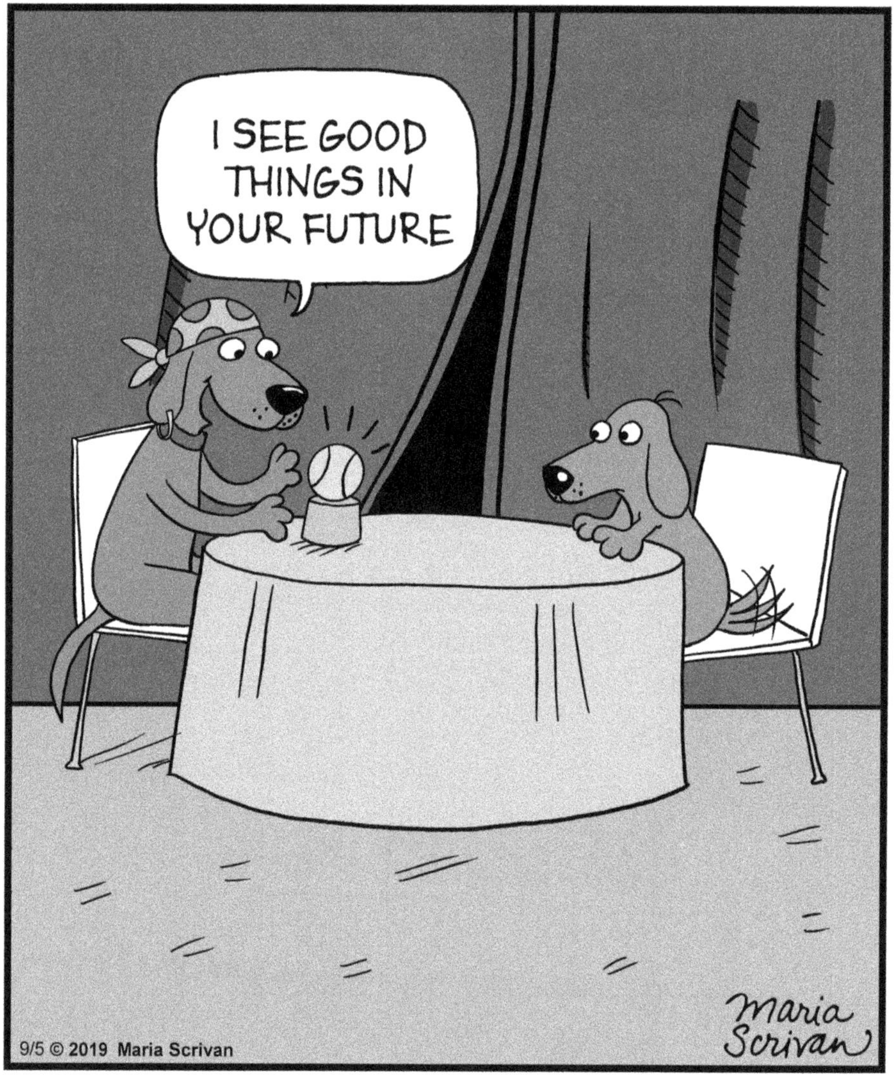
I SEE GOOD THINGS IN YOUR FUTURE
9/5 © 2019 Maria Scrivan
Maria Scrivan

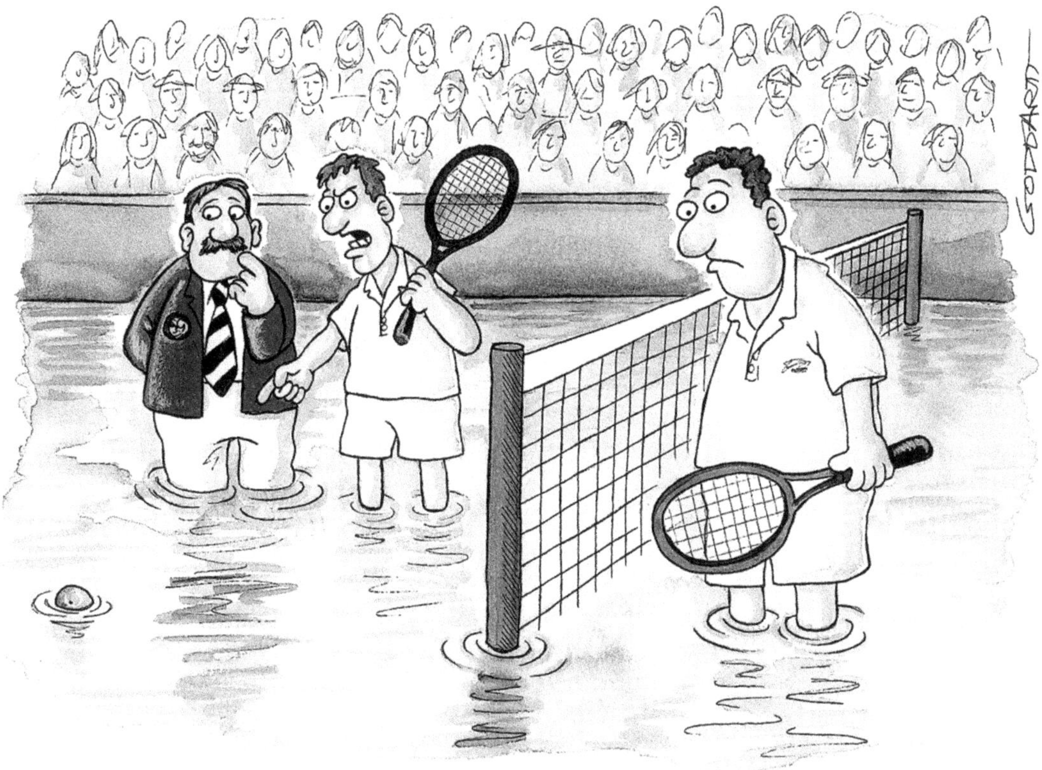
GODDARD

"Wimbledon - The British weather is causing ever more contentious line-calls."

MIXED DOUBLES

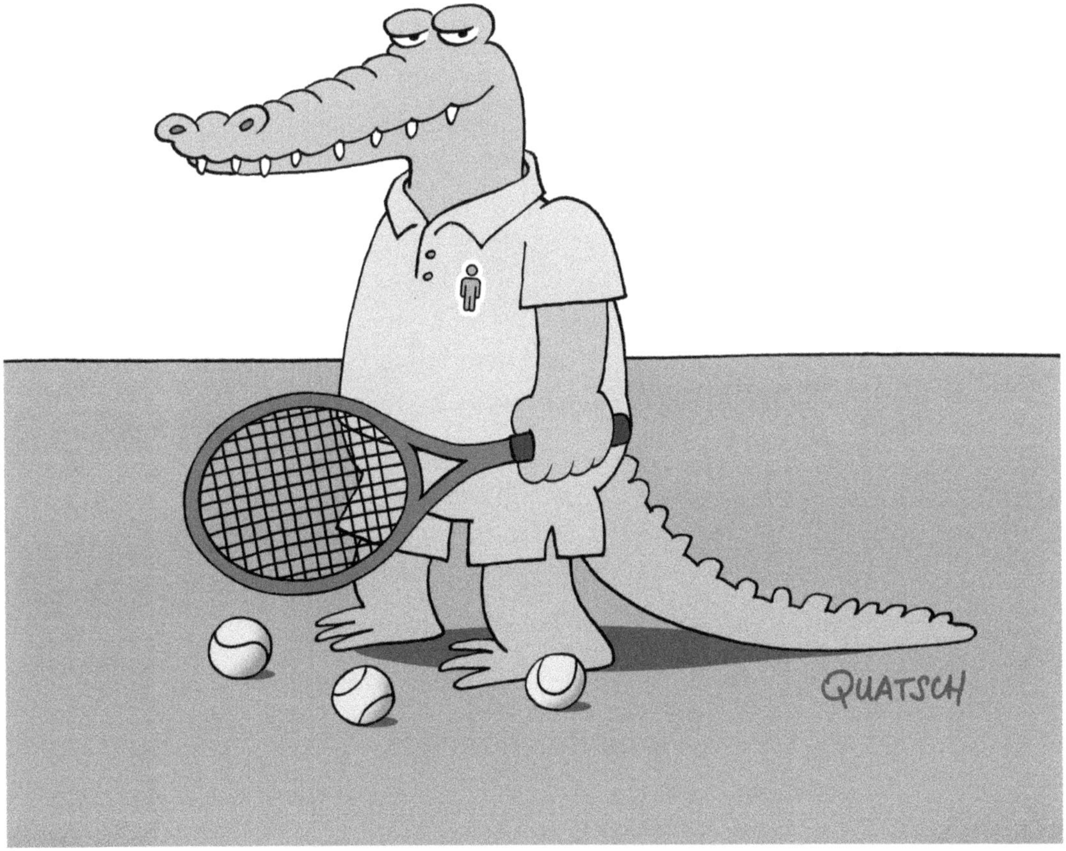
QUATSCH

"*Insurance, anyone?*"

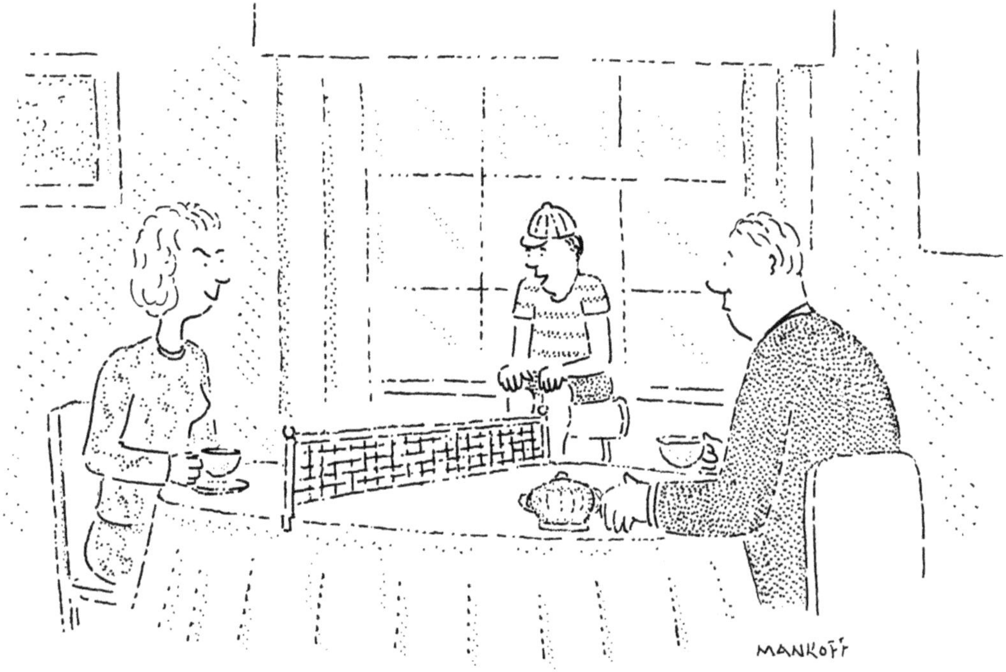
MANKOFF

"Advantage, Mom."

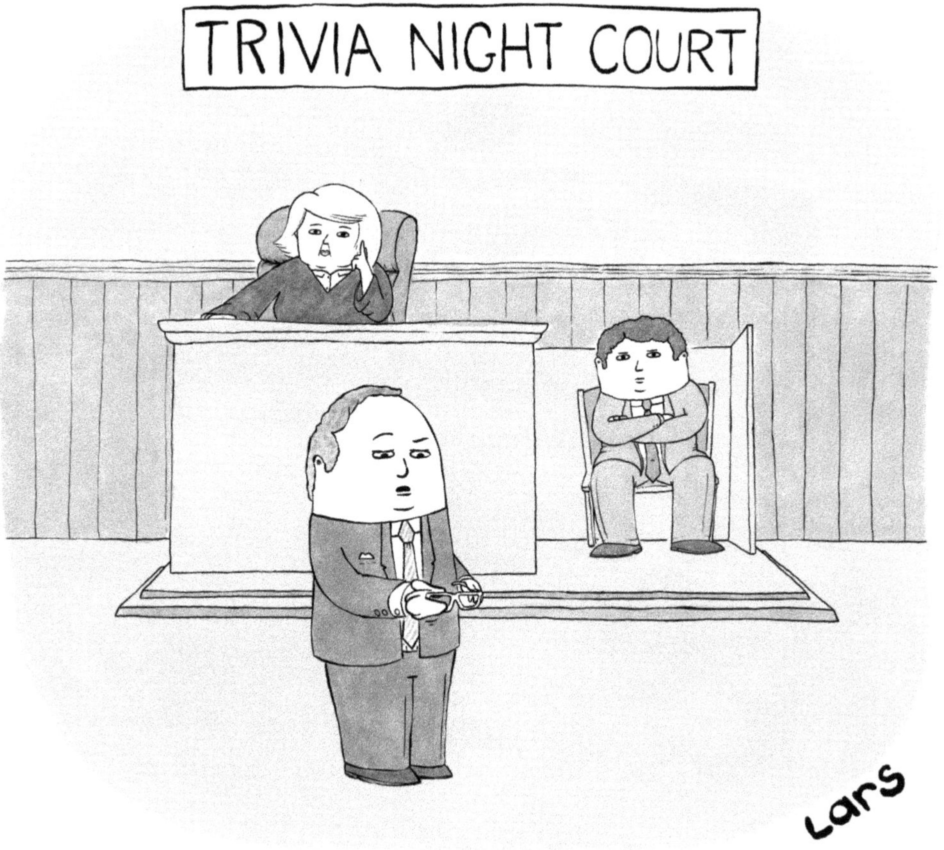
TRIVIA NIGHT COURT
Lars

"And on that fateful night, Mr. Gregson, do you recall how many times Bjorn Borg won Wimbledon?"

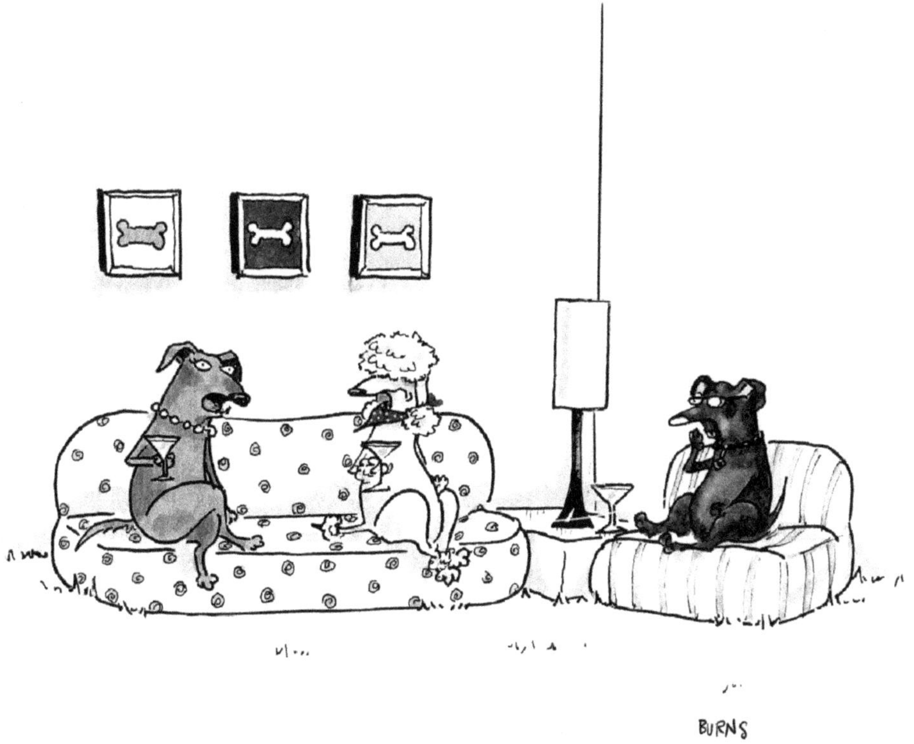
BURNS

"Yeah, well ***my*** *first husband left me for a tennis ball."*

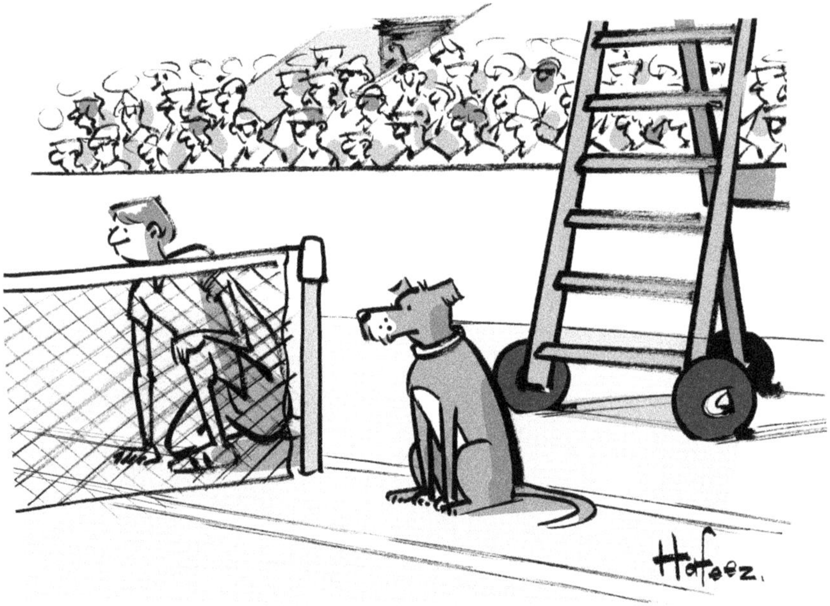
Hafeez.

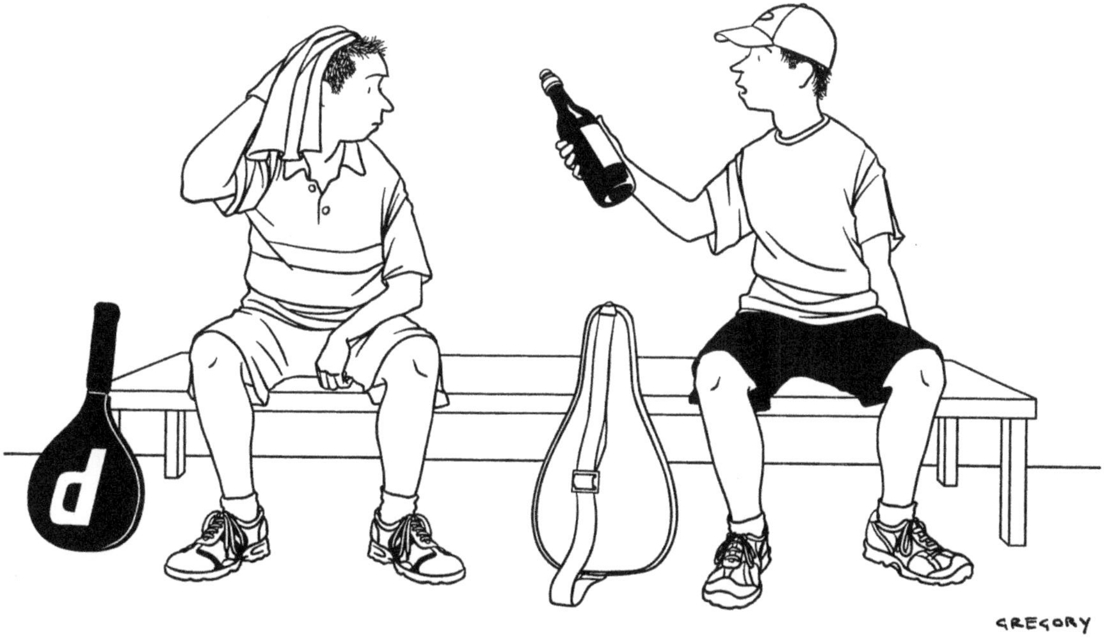
d
GREGORY

"Care for some sports wine?"

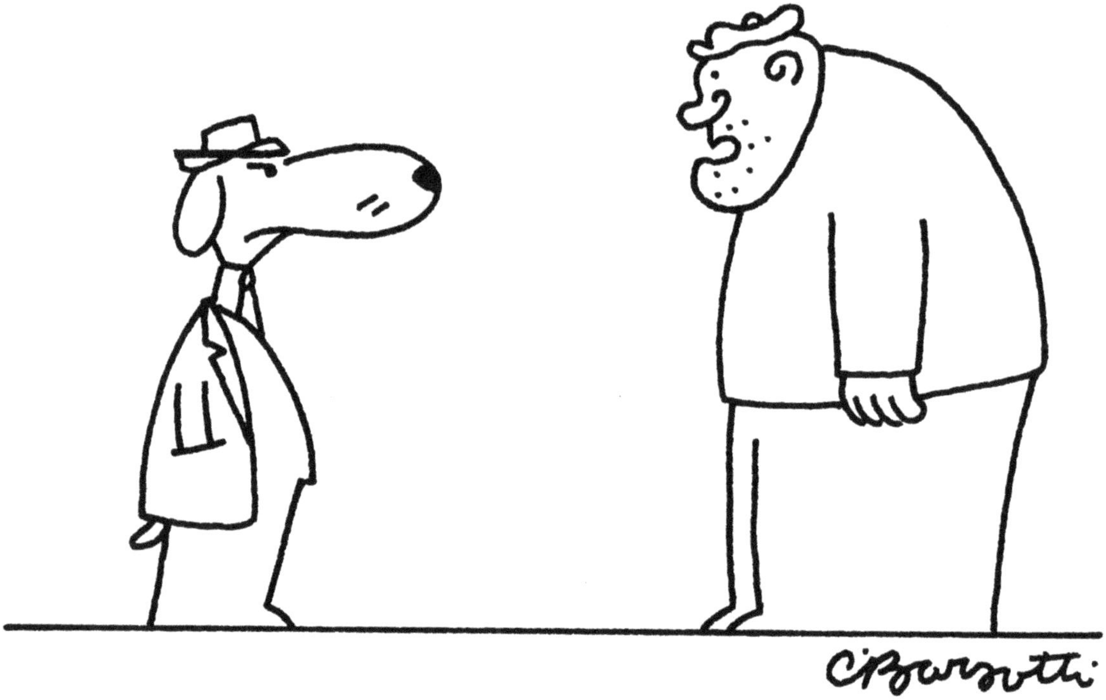
CBarsotti

"It looks bad, boss—they got your DNA off an old tennis ball."

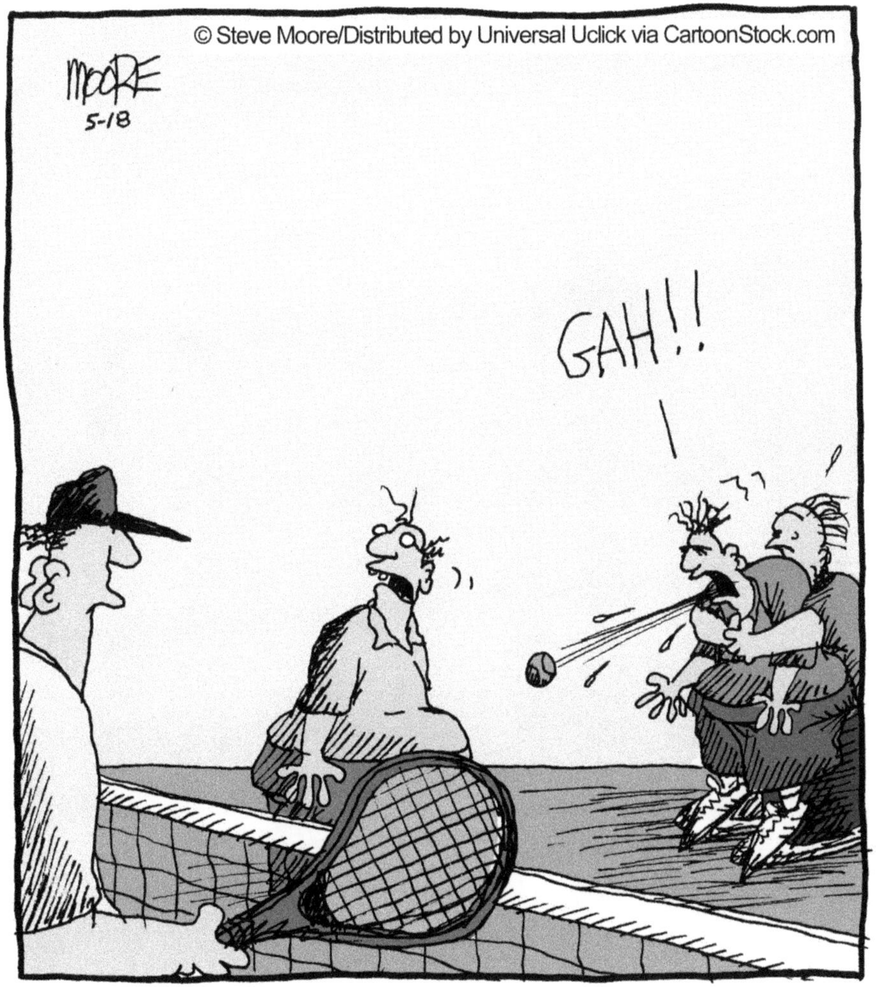
© Steve Moore/Distributed by Universal Uclick via CartoonStock.com
MOORE
5-18
GAH!!

"Wow. You've got a really powerful serve."

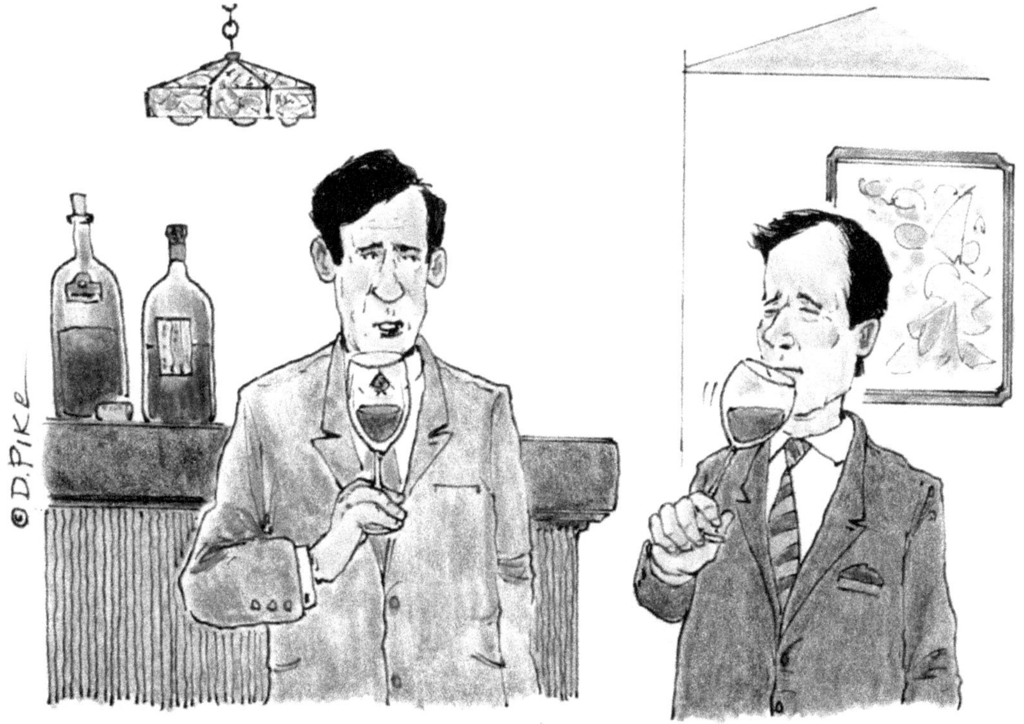
©D.PIKE

*"Hmmm...the aroma of tennis balls?
Hard court, or clay?"*

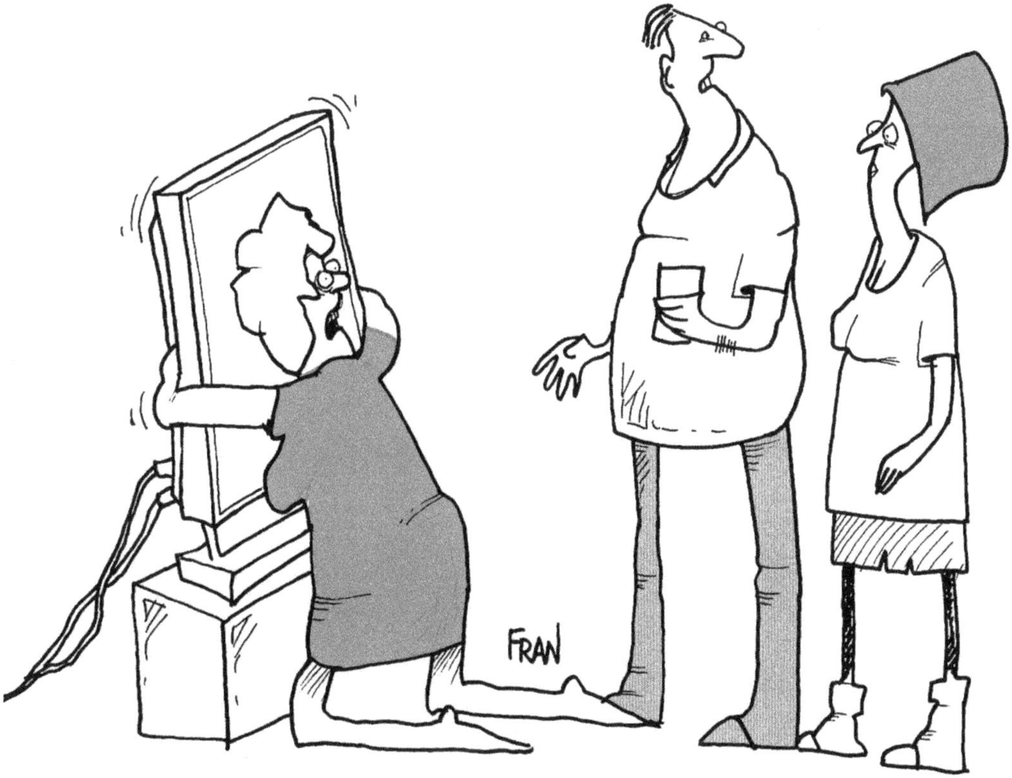
FRAN

"She's always like this when Wimbledon ends."

"I never finish them off right away. I like to play with the first."

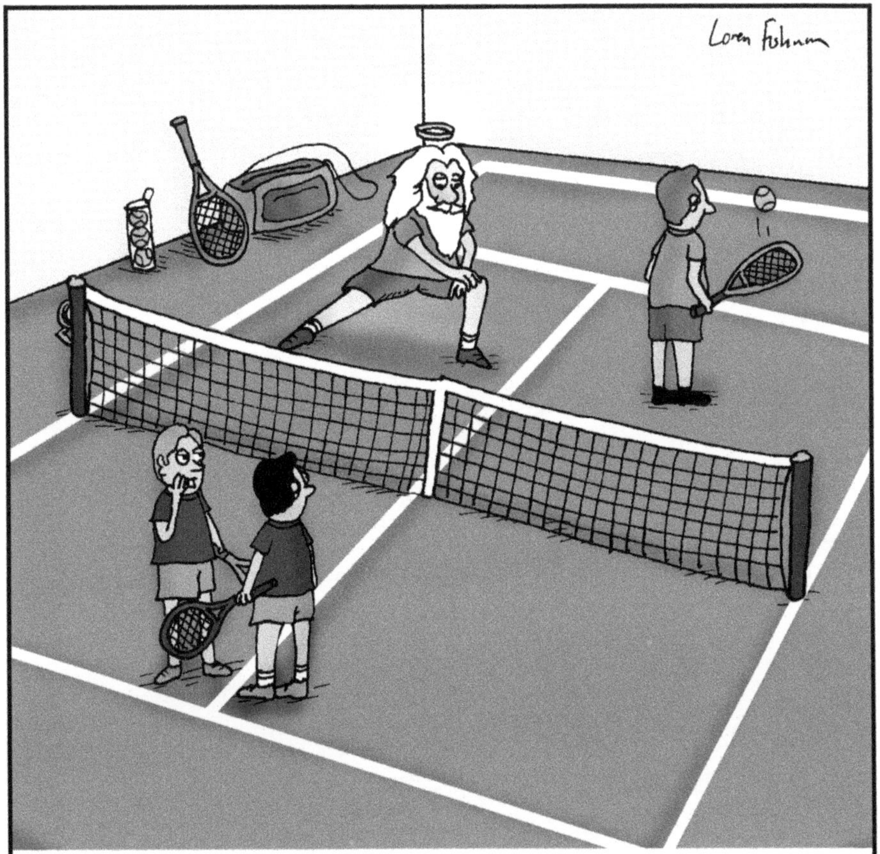
Loren Fishman

"Just don't get overconfident. This guy may not have much of a backhand, but he's got God on his side."

"It's better to keep the second ball in your pocket."

"He's been poaching for forty years
and she couldn't take it any more."

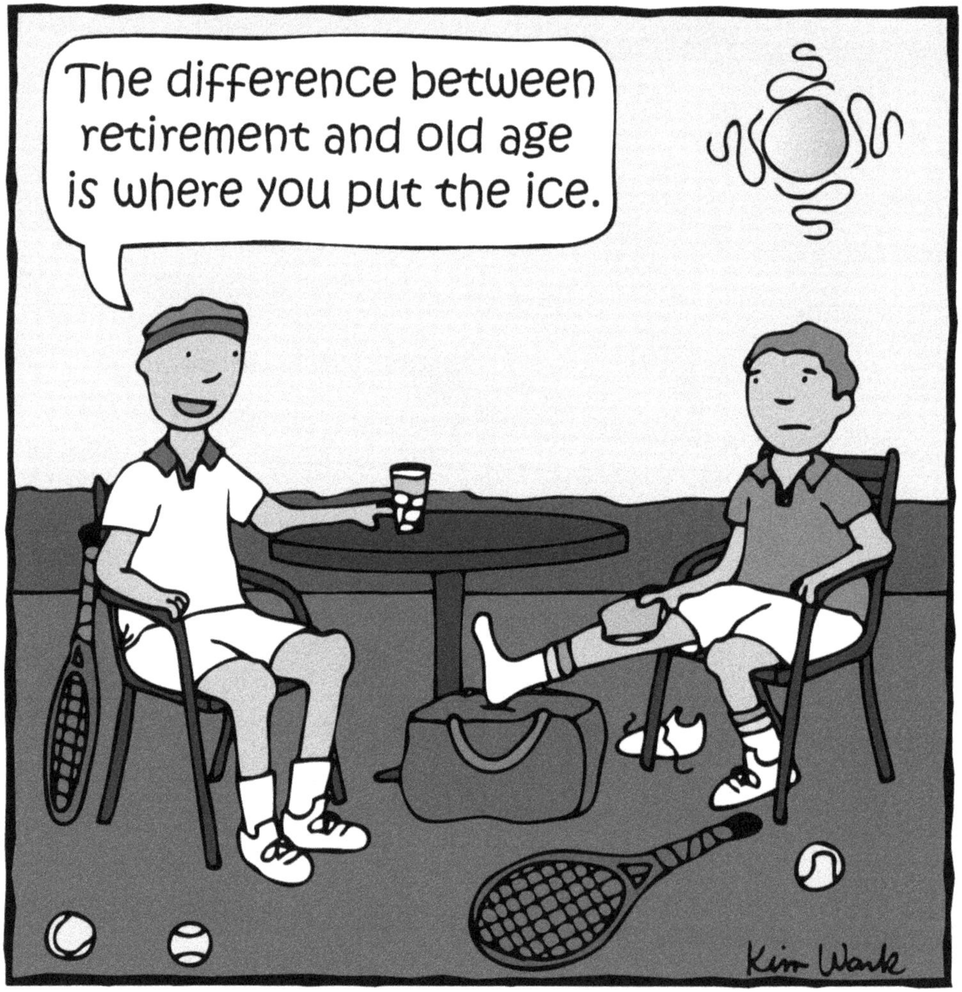
The difference between retirement and old age is where you put the ice.
Kim Warp

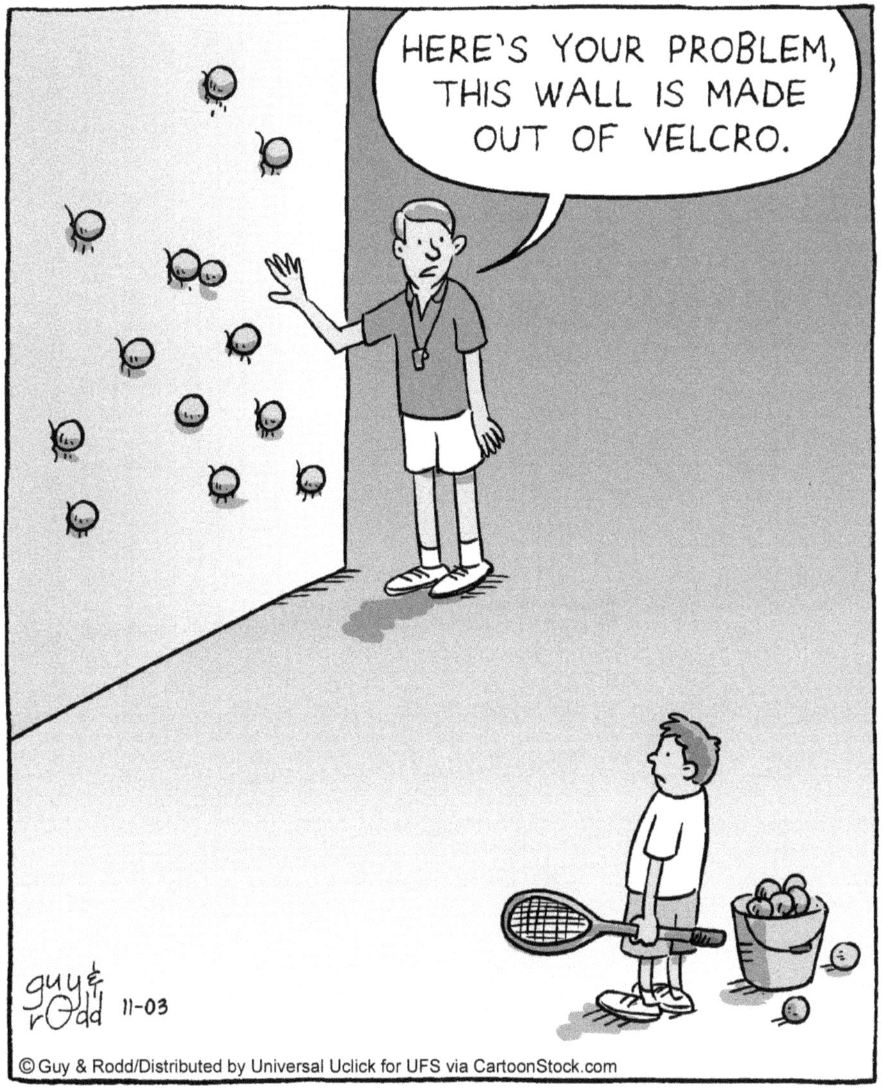
HERE'S YOUR PROBLEM, THIS WALL IS MADE OUT OF VELCRO.
guy & rodd 11-03
© Guy & Rodd/Distributed by Universal Uclick for UFS via CartoonStock.com

"Your serves are great. Ground strokes, superb. It's your foot faults that are killing you."

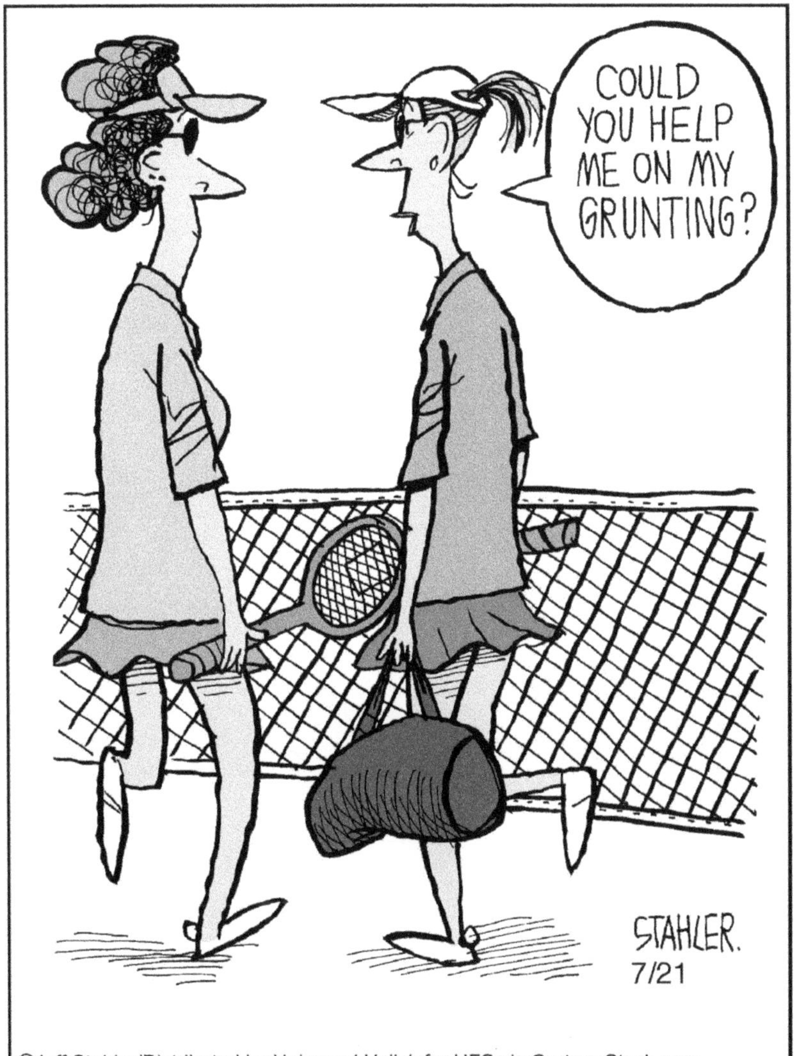
COULD YOU HELP ME ON MY GRUNTING?
STAHLER.
7/21

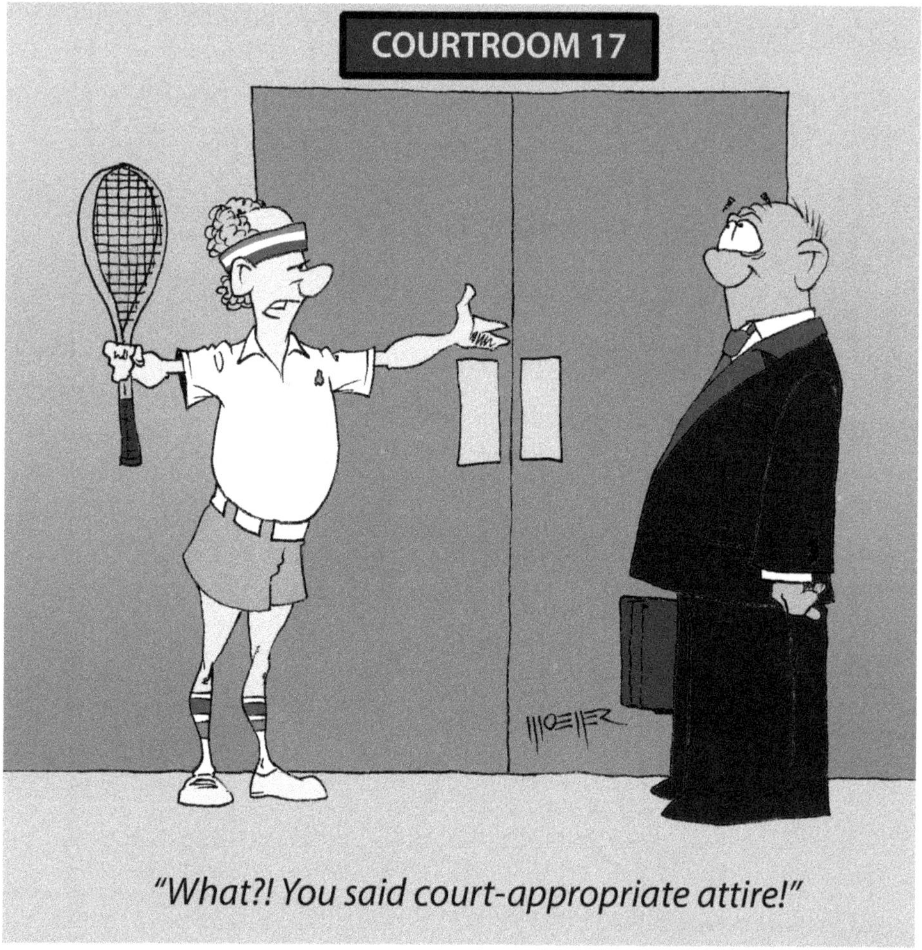
COURTROOM 17

"What?! You said court-appropriate attire!"

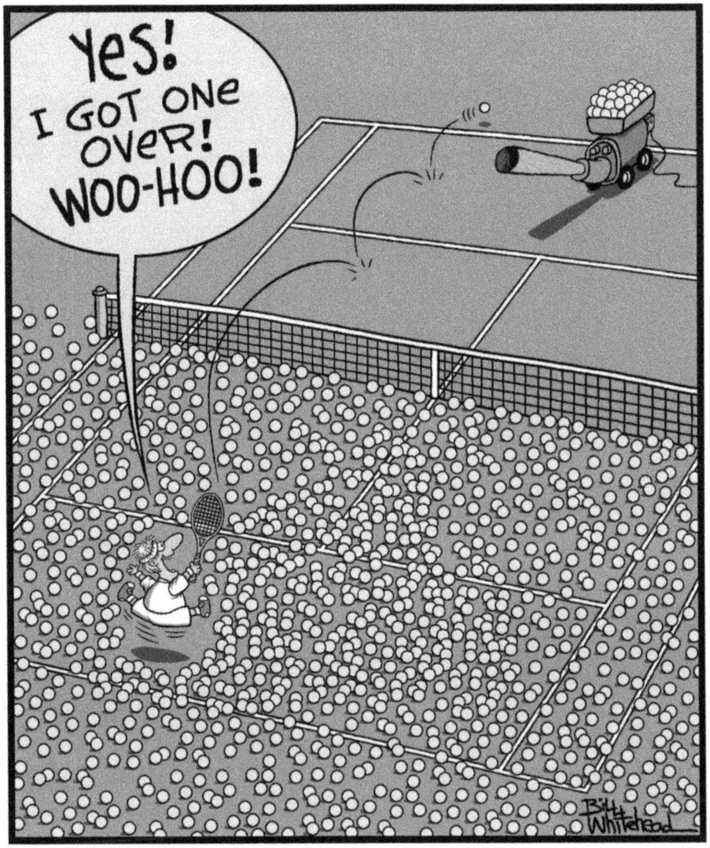
YES!
I GOT ONE
OVER!
WOO-HOO!
Bill
Whitehead

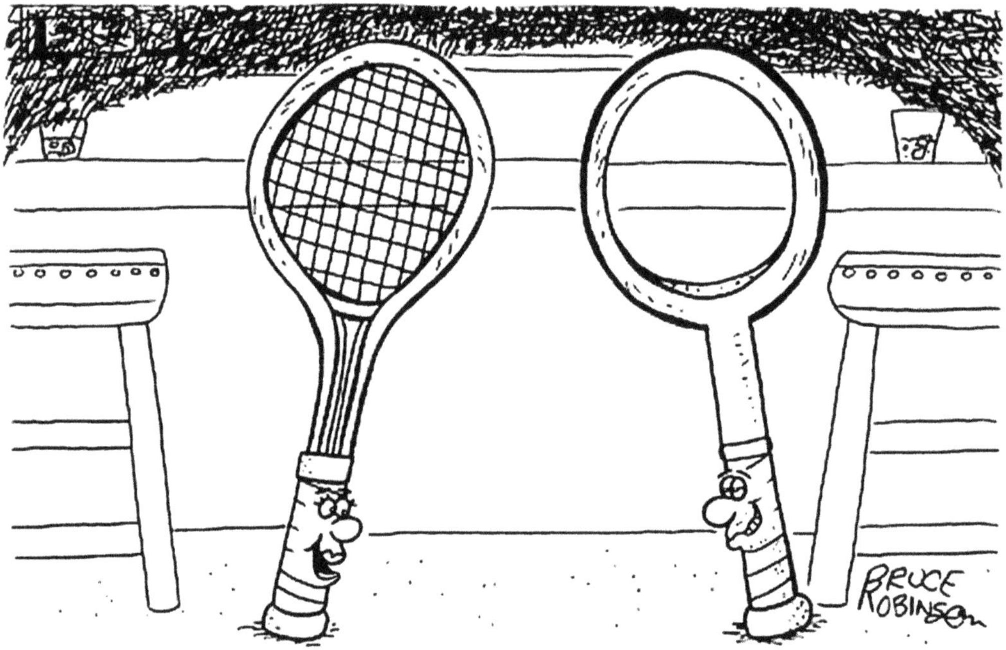
BRUCE
ROBINSON

"I've been looking for a relationship with no strings attached."

"Hmm, offhand, I'd say you have a
nasty case of tennis elbow!"

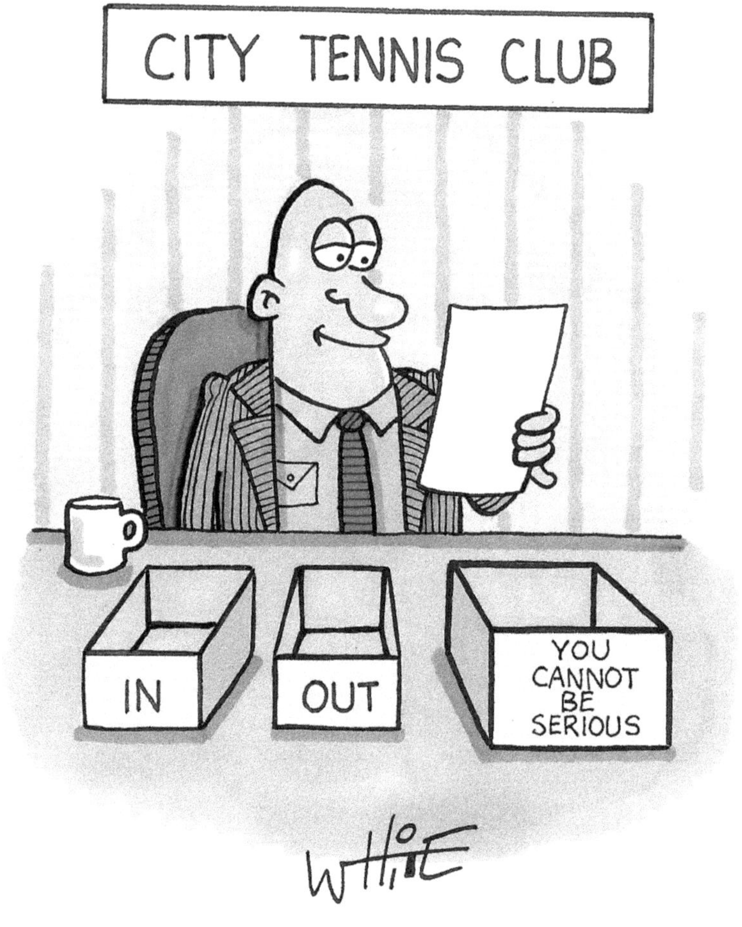
CITY TENNIS CLUB
IN
OUT
YOU CANNOT BE SERIOUS

Tennis Balls

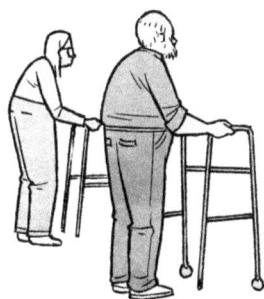

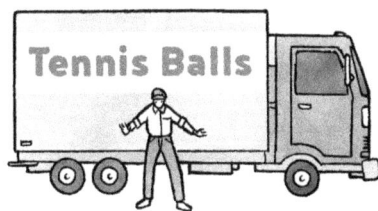

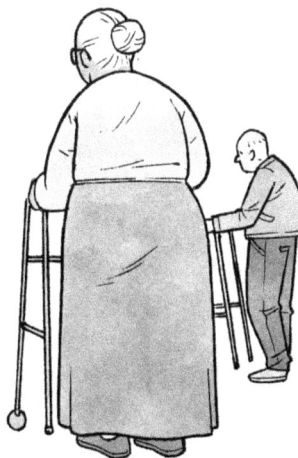

JON ADAMS

Index of Artists

www.ingramcontent.com/pod-product-compliance
Lightning Source LLC
Chambersburg PA
CBHW060759150426
42813CB00058B/2734
* 9 7 8 1 9 6 3 0 7 9 1 9 7 *